Spot the Spin

The FUN Way to Keep DEMOCRACY ALIVE & ELECTIONS HONEST

By Alan F. Kay

Note for Librarians: a cataloguing record for this
book that includes Dewey Classification and US
Library of Congress numbers is available from
the National Library of Canada. The complete
cataloguing record can be obtained from the
National Library's online database at:
www.nlc-bnc.ca/amicus/index-e.html
ISBN 1-4120-2547-8

Printed in Victoria, BC, Canada

TRAFFORD

**This book was published *on-demand* in
cooperation with Trafford Publishing.**
On-demand publishing is a unique process and
service of making a book available for retail sale
to the public taking advantage of on-demand
manufacturing and Internet marketing. **On-demand
publishing** includes promotions, retail sales,
manufacturing, order fulfilment, accounting and
collecting royalties on behalf of the author.

Suite 6E, 2333 Government St.,
Victoria, B.C. V8T 4P4, CANADA
Phone   250-383-6864
Toll-free   1-888-232-4444
Fax   250-383-6804
E-mail   sales@trafford.com
www.trafford.com/robots/04-0375.html

10   9   8   7   6   5   4   3   2   1

About the Author

Alan F. Kay, after a Harvard PhD in mathematics, co-founded a military research and development firm,1954-'63; founded and, 1966-'79, CEO of AutEx, supplier of "marketplace" systems to industry, the first B2B e-commerce company including pre-Internet email. (see www.autex.com)

In 1978 Alan, awakening to the sad state of politics and governance, became a self-employed donor and board member of policy organizations and an investor and no-charge advisor to start-up companies pioneering energy efficiency and anti-pollution technologies.

In 1987 his Americans Talk Issues (ATI) project, now part of the AH Foundation, established the art and science of public-interest polling (see www.publicinterestpolling.com). He is author of "*Locating Consensus for Democracy*", the book that founded public-interest polling. His web-based "Polling Critic" columns (see, www.cdi.org/polling), this book and numerous articles on business, democracy, and military topics focus on developing and supporting major social innovations (see www.alanfkay.com)

He is married, since 1996, to futurist, Hazel Henderson, has four grown sons, four grandchildren, and makes his home in Florida.

Table of Contents

Spot the Spin – The Fun Way to Keep Democracy Alive and Elections Honest

Chapter 1 Elites vs. the People – The 2004 Election

The Setting

Today we see elites with wealth and power dictating the course of government for their own benefit. The rest of us are getting a small and falling share of benefits. Even these often prove to benefit elites more than the people.

The purpose of the book is to present a viable and previously little-known way to make this country work well for everybody, not just for the well-heeled elites. This starts with spotting the spin elites put on information, now more visible every day. We can then demand honest high-quality public-interest polling which can reveal the public's true interest that is very different from the elites' spinning.

At stake are nothing less than improving our job opportunities, our environmental, health care, and educational systems, our approaches to national defense and security, and a government that truly serves the people.

Who are the elites?

At the top are a few thousand people:
- o A handful of powerful politicians and elected officials in Washington and in state governments.
- o Multi-millionaire investors and heads of very large corporations.
- o The moguls of the mainstream media, approximately the six largest media conglomerates.

A second level are many of the top lawyers, experts, accountants, pundits, campaign advisors, technicians, engineers, and many others who benefit mightily from catering to the wealth and power of the top elites.

The people are the rest of us – over ninety percent of the population of the US.

It's a World-Wide Problem

The disconnects between elites and the people, is a worldwide phenomenon. Most heads-of-state claim that majorities of their people approve of their policies and actions. Even dictators seek to legitimate their power based on similar claims. Opponents also claim that the people are with them. Who is right, leaders in power or opposition? Often, it turns out, neither. Large majorities of the general population worldwide have views different from leaders both in and out of power. This leads to enormous disconnects between the leaders and the led that are not alleviated as regime follows regime – even in democracies.

For example, polls conducted by GlobeScan, a UK company (formerly Environics, Toronto), in twenty countries around the world over the last five years have shown repeatedly that people everywhere want better education, health care and environmental protection. Yet governments spend more on the military and large projects of dubious value to ordinary people but financially rewarding to elites and special interests.

The Role of Public Interest Polling

There is only one practical way to find out what people want for governance: careful, high quality, scientific, random sample polling. Today in 60 countries there are pollsters who are capable of conducting such polls with remarkable accuracy. Why are their findings not better known?

One reason is that many polls are never made public – for example, those that leaders frequently commission to find out what to say to solidify their support. Secondly, a properly conducted, careful poll is labor-intensive and with 500 to 1500 interviews, too expensive for most purposes. Thirdly, polling is a competitive industry and commercial pollsters in all countries reflect the biases of their sponsors just to stay in business.

Furthermore, the mainstream news media, press, TV and radio, reflect the biases of their owners, advertisers, and political leaders in countries where they distribute or broadcast. This upstages findings from even the highest quality, most authoritative non-commercial polls that show the disconnect between leaders and public. This is especially true in the West, particularly the USA with its commercial "sound byte" news coverage.

The situation is not entirely hopeless. Sometimes commercial pollsters do high quality polls in the public interest. A few non-profit pollsters do so too – unfortunately with generally limited access to mass media. Public-interest polling often comes up with remarkably different results than those of the commercial firms such as Roper, Harris, Yankelovich, and, best known around the world, Gallup.

Political Fund Raising
One US development that has become increasingly clear to all in the last decade or two is that candidates for national and large state offices must raise prodigious amounts of money for their election and re-election campaigns from wealthy financial backers who openly expect to be rewarded by legislation and regulations favorable to themselves in amounts much larger than what they shell out for election campaigns.

If, as it appears, a quarter of a billion dollars is now the cost of winning a presidential election, all financial backers as a group will easily get returns from the new president's administration in the range of 2 to 20 billion dollars worth of benefits: reduced taxes; low cost loans; juicy government contracts; approvals of lucrative mergers and acquisitions; and even perks like overnights in the Lincoln bedroom. Most sponsors of lobbying and large campaign contributors look at their contributions as investments that can pay-off 10 to1, 100 to 1, and even more.

The Crisis of the 2004 Election
The rewards to those who wink at, or quietly pay for, corruption of the election process to assure that their guy or their party wins is so large that it is only realistic to expect much more massive fraud in future elections than we have ever seen before. This is especially true for 2004, when large numbers of votes can be voided, miscounted, uncounted, disappeared, or transformed by software quietly embedded in touch-screen voting machines, many in the 2004 election with no written record of the ballot cast that is essential if a recount is required. If no recount can be justified, then the existence of the paper trail is of no use, except to prove, long after the election is over, that justice miscarried, as happened in Florida 2000.

Florida 2000 might look like a small-scale dress rehearsal in hindsight. In 2004 there will be dozens of different types of voting machines that will have to be programmed or set up just before election with data: candidate names, offices, instructions, etc., almost unique to each of the 200,000 precinct voting places, because the voting for local offices too takes place on election-day. About two weeks is all the time available for programming or setting up the two million voting machines necessary for a nationwide vote in one day. To find and prevent the small amount of fraud in a few key states that is needed to swing a close election is more difficult than finding a needle in a giant haystack covering the entire country. The oversight to do this all on election-day does not exist. National, election-day voting and vote-counting is a unique activity unlike any other computerized or partially computerized process that the US has ever dealt with.

There are ways to overcome all of this eventually. See for example http://www.alanfkay.com/National%20Elections.htm. But all of the problems mentioned above cannot be solved by Nov 2004. 2004 is the hump we have to get over to re-secure democracy.

Political Spinning Leads to Lying and the End of Democracy
Spin is melded into politicians' appearances, speeches, and remarks; more spin is added by advisors and handlers; and further spin comes from the mainstream media. The revenue of TV, radio, newspapers, and magazines comes largely from advertising that is designed to maximize product sales and focus attention on the positive aspects of the product, the brand, or the company that is paying the freight. Fair, balancing views of the product/service are excluded from commercials and print ads. The results are unfair and unbalanced ads that ubiquitously lie by omission. Enough spinning by candidates, advisors, and media finally becomes nothing less than lying. Lying by omission works surprisingly well for politicians with the cooperation of the mainstream media. By the time the country catches up with a lie shrouded in secrecy, officials have gotten the benefits they seek from running the government, and so far, seem to pay little or no price for degrading the voice of the people, and corrupting the democratic process. If the electorate does not know the pertinent facts, the people cannot make wise decisions on election-day.

It is no exaggeration to say that democracy hangs by a thread.

Resolving the Crisis

Learning to spot the spin in political polling, helps us understand what high quality public-interest polling can do to make you and ultimately all people understand the consensus of the public's view of issues. The elites would prefer that the public not know the public's true views. When in power they keep secret anything that shows the weakness of their policies and the poverty of their choices. Spotting the spin is the first step in reclaiming true democracy.

If you are ready to learn how easily you can spot the spin in political polls, read on.

Chapter 2 The Basics for Telling a Good Poll from a Bad Poll

So you would like to spot the spin. You want to know how to tell a good poll from a bad poll, to see examples of the confusion caused by misleading polls. Well, why not? We all need a little help to tell the good from the bad, and there is much more to be said about good and bad polling than is ever told us by the media – newspapers, news magazines, radio, the Internet and TV.

After devoting fifteen or twenty years of my life to non-profit polling in the public interest, I've never once been involved in the polling business commercially. This book is about what I learned from the inside of US politics. You are about to become an expert in detecting bias – whether from politicians, bureaucrats, company pr flacks, academics, media pundits, or pollsters. You will become a master at spotting spinmasters and their spin.

My involvement in public interest polling started. long ago. In 1946 I was a twenty year old interpreter in the US occupation forces, having learned Japanese in the army at the University of Minnesota. In Tokyo I did "man on the street" interviews for MacArthur that provided the old general with feedback that contributed to the remarkable reconstruction of Japan. In 1945 Japan was a destroyed totalitarian dictatorship. In a few years it became a free, democratic, market-loving country. Do I believe in the value of good polling to help transform a country for the better? You bet.

What is a good poll and what is a bad poll? Some people take a narrow view. Looking at a poll result in the paper or hearing one over the air, a good poll is a poll that pleases them. They like it even better if a large majority agrees with them. A bad poll is one whose findings they don't like and they prefer not to know or think about. We can do better!

In this book a good poll is one where the sponsor (the one who pays the freight) is honestly trying to find out -- and trying to let the public know -- what the public itself thinks and wants, not what the public thinks and wants as explained by the pundits – those talking heads on TV who seem to know everything. A public interest poll truly has the public's interest at heart, rather than a poll commissioned by a public relations firm or anyone trying to push a particular product, cause, or political viewpoint.

A bad poll is one where those paying for it want the public to believe that the public wants what those paying want. It is not the case that in a given poll all the questions are either good or bad. There may be many good questions in a bad poll. Among the polls the public gets to see, there are very few *really good* polls. Because of various checks and balances we'll talk about later, most polls are *pretty good*. But how can an ordinary person, like most of us are, tell the difference between polls that are really good, pretty good, bad, and terrible?

Usually, really good polls are an honest and unbiased attempt to explore the public's view, scientifically and even if they are surprised or dismayed by the results publish them truthfully. The worst polls try to confirm the biases of the organization or politician who's paying for them and seek to manipulate the public and engineer consent for their pet policies or sell their products.

My small foundation, Americans Talk Issues (ATI) spent fourteen years polling the American people – over the heads of the politicians and pollsters – to find out what policies they really wanted. We published poll results in all of these issue areas: the national budget, national security, energy, trade, the environment, globalization and government reform, in the book *Locating Consensus for Democracy*, ATIF 1998. Now, here in this handbook I've culled out the most important insights that every citizen needs to know to make the US democratic system work better for the people – rather than for the special interests.

This book will be your tour guide through the polling business and its clients and give you some easy ways to tell a good poll question from a bad one, a good poll from a bad one, and to distinguish the good guy sponsors from the bad guy sponsors. Not all the ways are easy. Some require more detective work. Readers may enjoy the challenge. If you get bored or confused, skim the section and go on to the next. There will be no test.

We'll see that people who sponsor polls and those who conduct them are pretty smart. After all, those not making six figure incomes in the polling business, are not really trying. They are generally savvy people. Still the baddies often leave tell-tale signs of poll-rigging, and I'll show you how to spot them. And then every once in a while, you'll find out about a very big, bad guy who falls facedown on the floor and loses his place in the political game.

There are a few basic things that must be said about polling. The first is that in a vast sea of polls, the public sees only the tips of the icebergs. Looking only above the waterline, there are three kinds of polls that the public learns about. The first are the polls that the news media put out. As the editors of the New York Times and the Washington Post have told me, the stories newspapers cover are just those that their readers are interested in. In other words, the mainstream media try to tell us that they conduct polls to satisfy their readers' thirst for knowledge. Is this what really happens?

Mainstream newspaper readers are tracked in the advertising, circulation and subscription departments, which have a lot to say to the editorial department about what their reader counts and earnings figures are telling them about reader interest. It is not hard to see that this means that the media chooses to run polls that beef up stories, features, and news items in order to, well, help sell papers or advertising.

The editorial people don't think that way. They will be insulted if you tell them what I have just told you. But they don't see the big picture outside of their daily grind. I have been scorned when I tried to explain to them years ago how it works. But the bottom line is clear. Poll findings do not get placed in print, radio, or TV in order to educate the news consumer.

I once asked Kathy Frankovic, head of polling for CBS, why media pollsters never ran polls on what the people thought about eras that were ending. What lessons did we learn from seminal events like the end of the Vietnam war or the collapse of the Soviet Union? The people paid a lot in energy, casualties and tax money in these long term efforts. Was it worth it? Could a better outcome have been achieved in another way? Kathy's answer was, "We don't do social research." What the mainstream news media think is that what the people themselves want is not news. How the people *react* to

10   –Ch.2–

what *political leaders* want is their definition of news. These are how many distortions and misperceptions arise in our political debates.

In big election years, media polling takes on another character. Most of the polling budget for those years goes for covering the campaigns like horse-races or battles, full of war metaphors and brutal sport analogies. It's all about what the politicians want – in this case obvious – to be elected, and what the media want, a good, exciting story. The two work together, hand in glove.

Elections are conducted and media poll questions pop up asking voters who they want elected. But we the people have little real choice. The only candidates who can get national media attention have paid a high price for that rise to prominence. In the end it's "Do you prefer tweedledum or tweedledee?" This is not to say that sometimes one is not better than the other. During the campaign most voters see a big difference between tweedle*dum* and tweedle*dee*. But once *dum* gets into office, the pressure is the same on him as it was on *dee*. The public's needs get the bum's rush in *dum*'s rush to please the top elites.

People who go into politics to do the right thing often get weeded out. Their campaign funds dry up. Most political newcomers convert to mastering the back-scratching techniques needed to stay in the game and rise to power. They also master the art of convincingly explaining to a skeptical public that everything they do is in the public interest. In fact, a weary and disillusioned US electorate is beginning to believe that power-hungry, ego-driven politicians together with the money from special interest backers rarely serve the public interest.

When the public was asked in a poll question, 64% agreed that they "preferred that the politicians they vote for hold higher and more evolved moral and ethical values than they do", and if that doesn't impress you, keep in mind that most people have convinced themselves that their ethics suits them fine.

The second kind of poll that people get to see are those that are sponsored by policy organizations and foundations, some large regulars like Pew Charitable Trust, the Kaiser Family foundation, the Democratic and Republican parties and AARP and many less affluent non-profits that occasionally scrape up the money needed to do a poll. There are also a few polling organizations that conduct occasional polls designed in-house and conducted both for promotion of their name and as a public service. Do these non-media polls have spin? Yes, sometimes.

Finally there are a few pollsters affiliated with universities, syndicators of poll findings, and independent non-profits, who truly poll in the public interest. How can you tell how pure they are? We'll see how sponsors choose to fight spin, accept it, or depend upon it for their purposes.

Now, let's look below the waterline at the extent of the icebergs and why there are so many of them. Polling is a good business. Top commercial pollsters earn six figure incomes cranking out polls that good customers want. A good customer is one who will plunk down $100,000 or more for a typical poll. For that kind of money the customer gets a scientific random-sample of a thousand telephone or in-person interviews and, most important, the reliability and professionalism of the pollster who can assure them that the poll findings will be credible and satisfy their needs.

There is one kind of customer that regularly spends that kind of money. Corporations, the great bulk of polling firms' clients, do so much polling that they have been able to squeeze prices way down. Still commercial market research is a gigantic $40 billion/yr. business, most of which goes into surveying to find out what the public wants for products and services.

A chunk of that dollar is for unscientific, but much liked, studies using focus groups. A facilitator guides a dozen or so people sitting around a table for a couple of hours discussing whether they would buy various versions of a new dog food, a different kind of life insurance plan, or an improved SUV. Sometimes researchers look in through one-way glass or observe a screened replay. The group is more-or-less randomly selected to represent the particular public segment that the sellers believe is a broad view of their potential market. A good facilitator can ferret out what is behind individual preferences. The information can be very valuable and so is considered proprietary by the companies to keep their competitors in the dark.

Of course, the findings of corporate-sponsored random sample polls are top secret too. The public never sees the results. Even though this kind of poll is the most numerous by far, the public hardly knows that such polls exist and are the bread-and-butter of commercial polling organizations.

Commercial polling is 98% market research and less than two percent political polling. You'll see the effects of the market research on political polling. Marketeers are responsible for spending what adds up to a national $200 billion annual ad budget. Large corporations selling directly to the public, like car manufacturers, fast food franchisers, brand name apparel designers, hospitality chains, jewelry chains, media mogul empires, etc., launch multimillion dollar ad campaigns and the money from their point of view is seldom wasted. They have our number, don't they? We the public are scrutinized by direct mail firms, advertisers, TV ratings or Internet snoopers who "data mine" our purchase records, and place "cookies" on our computer hard-drives. We are surrounded.

If you are a top pollster and most of your work is for marketeers, you give them what they want to know: how to describe their wares so that more people and more upscale people will buy them. When commercial market research pollsters take over the job of satisfying political candidates, they naturally think in terms of selling them the way they sold corn flakes. Package the politicians up like toothpaste and sell the public on them. Don't misunderstand. Pollsters are smart, skilled, and know their business. Manufacturers only want to sell what they make or might consider making. So pollsters have to help marketeers find the right new "product" too: new issues that may be "hot" or putting the required spin on old issues or slanting emerging news stories.

Political pollsters and campaign strategists trying to find out how to sell their candidates face one key factor that is different from market research polling. If requested they have to stay with the client they agree to represent and hope to get him or her elected. If they leave because the client isn't selling (after all, at least half the candidates in a competitive race don't get elected), no one will want to hire them again. In the political field there is no "manufacturer of candidates" who can make a new candidate during a campaign, if the old one isn't selling. When commercial pollsters accept the occasional political candidate or even when they specialize in political polling as a few do, their mindset doesn't change from the straight commercial one.

Another important thing to know about polling is this. It's all about numbers. Are you are a number person? Who is? Rest easy. You are not alone. The good news is that the only thing you need to know about numbers in polling is easier than learning how to make change for a dollar. I never met anyone on the street who couldn't do that – usually better than I can. Come to think of it, seeing the significance of numbers in polling is a lot like counting change. But first basics.

We all know how to recognize blatant bias in polling with the proverbial "Have you stopped beating your wife" question. Another wise maxim is "Ask a silly question and you'll get a silly answer." Computers have taught us a similar maxim, "Garbage in, garbage out." But we can sharpen up the essence of the problem in polling that occurs even with the simplest "yes" or "no" questions. In such questions the verb is often "agree or disagree", "approve or disapprove" or slightly more complicated "favor A or favor B". In such questions there seem to be two choices, one or the other. Even if the question is simply, "Do you favor A?", and no B is mentioned there is a choice of "no". In this case, B is just "not A". Still there is a small problem – with lots of consequences. There is always a third choice and sometimes many more.

How often have you tried to respond to a telephone poll and found such yes/no choices absurd? If you hung up, good for you. You or the person taking the poll – called the respondent, "R", can respond with, "I dunno" or maybe not respond at all. It happens. The pollster doing the interview would ultimately of course give up and hang up, but more likely, the interviewer goes to the next question and often begins to get real answers from R. Of course, R can say other more articulate things, like "I just don't know" or "I won't/can't answer that". These "no answer" or non-substantive replies are just lumped together in a "Don't Know" or DK bin, whose contents in most survey reports are called the DKs.

Now it is also possible for R to be more assertive, saying things like, " I object to the biased way you have formulated this question. I neither approve nor disapprove" Such an R is not very cooperative from the interviewer's point of view. But that is only a mild version of the problem. For the full problem, imagine the question asks R to choose between favoring choice A or choice B – two more-or-less opposite choices. The real problem then turns out to be the most cooperative and knowledgeable R, who might say something like this.

"You ask me if I favor A or B. Well here is my honest answer. I favor A -- under conditions X (skip the details of what X is. R could take a few hundred words to do it justice!). It gets worse. R goes on. "I favor B – under conditions Y. I favor neither A nor B under conditions Z, and I favor both A and B under conditions W". With X, Y, Z, and W running into hundreds of words each, our know-it-all R has just burned up five minutes, and the interviewer cannot use a word of it, because he can only point and click his CATI (Computer Assisted Telephone Interviewing) monitor for A or B or Don't Know, the three "codes" that CATI has been pre-programmed to accept.

Look, I've listened to hundreds of interviews on a receive-only monitor phone and I have heard Rs who say much of this. I have never heard anyone actually say all of this, but it is theoretically possible. The point is, to respect the public's intelligence, poll questions should embrace the widest possible range of choices in responding to questions not having yes/no choices – which are always coercive.

Now the basics are over. Here is where the numbers come in. CATI keeps a running count of all those who have chosen each of the allowed choices – as we saw at least three for every question. When the survey is completed, CATI divides the counts by the number who were asked the question and gives us percentages, such as:

A: favored by 32%, B: favored by 64%, DK is 4% -- which adds to 100% of those who were asked the question.

This is like putting change of a dollar into three piles: 32¢ in one pile, 64¢ in another, and 4¢ in the third. It adds to a dollar.

Now, I promised you it would be simpler than making change. Here is how.

When we pile up those pennies we have to get them right or someone will complain. But in random-sample polling there is a certain inaccuracy related to how many people completed the poll. You don't need to know about any of that. The exact way pollsters calculate this statistical inaccuracy is used to keep people who don't understand it from playing in the polling game. Pollsters are very careful to handle this problem accurately and all you have to know is that the so-called sampling error in random sample polls allows you to not have to treat the numbers as sacred or very accurate. Pollsters choose the sample size to be somewhere between 700 and a thousand (rarely as much as 2000) and that turns out to mean mathematically that there may be an error but it is probably less than 4 pennies in the pile with 64 pennies, less than 3 pennies for the pile with 22 pennies and 1 penny in the pile of 4 pennies. It would hardly be any more accurate if the polling sample had 1500 people who took the poll. Larger sample size does not help that much.

An important thing to know is that even the worst polls do not muff this point, because it is the first thing that anyone looks at before they take a poll seriously. The spin, as we will see, is much more obscure than cheating on sample size.

The key thing that the expensive poll reveals are those percentage numbers. That is the main value produced from the $100,000 cost of the poll. Yes, the percentage responses are not perfectly accurate, but accurate enough for political purposes, and no one is going to argue over them, except academics trying to make sure that PhD candidates know all about sample size, how to calculate it, and what it really means. We will talk no more about sample size or statistical errors, except to say here how unimportant they may be.

A common situation is that two different policy proposals differ in their favorability rating by only 1 (yes, one) percentage point. Then it is also true that the more highly rated one is more likely to be favored than the less highly rated among the whole population, say all adults over 18, regardless of the sample size. Of course, the same is even more true if their difference is 2%, 3% or more. With a difference above 3% and the sample size above about 700, then even the academics will usually agree that the difference is significant enough to assert it *as if it were a fact*. That's fine, but it misses a valuable aspect. It is amazing how useful the idea that these small differences (as small as 1 percent) that admittedly are not definitive still can provide very helpful clues in systematic searching for the policies people most prefer. The academics hate the idea, not only because it sidesteps all the highbrow mathematics they have mastered, but also first because it works in practical searches and second because understanding it just requires common sense. No university can give out PhDs for common sense.

We need to perfect our democracy. Ordinary people get paid for hard work. We play by the rules and we're busy and involved in our own daily lives. We are a large quiet majority. We do not have the time or energy to focus on the complexities of why and how we are not getting what we want and need from big government. When we look closely at all the players, we begin to see that it is the System that forces all of us, including politicians and moguls, to play the roles that the System itself seems to require for us to play. For now, getting the money out of politics is an important goal to help politicians to see how little attention they pay to what the overwhelming majority of us want and should have. In time other benign ways to transform the System will emerge and become apparent to those of us who think about these things. Please join in and learn how to make your life more meaningful by helping others in ways that will help all of us including you and every other person on the planet get the governance we want, need, and should have.

Chapter 3. Spin -- From the Media -- Via the Media

News comes through the media. Whether it's TV or print, the media mediates. It hovers over all the regular news sources and stands between the people and news information. If not covered by the media then it is not news. If it wasn't on TV, it did not happen.

The Internet, where millions of people can publish news to the world, to some degree is breaking the media monopoly. But news content coming over the Internet is almost entirely provided by the mainstream media courtesy of Microsoft. Exceptions are a few citizen's organizations, like MoveOn and TrueMajority, that despite established media indifference and rejection can fund candidates like Howard Dean or flood Congress with several hundred thousand emails.

Before we look at the spin put on polls, we have to see how spin is put on all news and current affairs content by the decision makers of the media using media channels. There are a large number of different ways to put spin on poll findings. In this book, we'll look at some that are easy to understand and unique and ingenious. Most of them, however, are similar to the ways that the media put spin on any subject they touch.

If you're a typical American you've already put in over ten thousand hours in front of our most important source of news, TV. That's over a year's time for an all-out 24x7x52 marathon. For the younger crowd, the number is even higher if you include time in front of on-line TV monitors. Most of us have learned a lot from the experience. Even if most of those hours strictly speaking are not in front of news or current affairs, directly or indirectly, a lot of it is. Whether your favorite news media comes via print, TV, or the Internet, you probably know a lot about media spin and perhaps many of the things you'll read here.

Much of the spinning hides behind the double protection of the first amendment, freedom of speech and freedom of the press. "Freedom of the press is only for those who own one", is just as accurate an aphorism today as it was fifty years ago when fast distribution of high-circulation news required giant lithographic presses. Today owning your own mainstream media is only for a handful of moguls. A TV channel costs over $100 million and even buying a small local station is for the very upscale and entrepreneurial. Want to buy a major newspaper? Better be ready to shell out over a billion. With very few exceptions, the owners of media outlets use them to promote their own ideas. Some are blatantly, ideologically biased and totally devoted to their own viewpoints. Some allow and indeed encourage more balanced viewpoints. Large audience and mainstream media usually seem balanced. Much of that may be an illusion.

How come? Much of the content picked up and carried in mainstream media has been designed and built around the ways and means of spinning stories. Much of it comes off of PR newswire or other release services whereby the key participants in a news story, the newsmakers or corporate management, tell the story *their* way, or from government as when the US Department of Health and Human Services put out Video News Releases (VNRs) on the 2003 Medicare Act that were "spun" in ways so blatant that they were legally challenged as using government funds for political propaganda. The bias is there, and usually subtle.

Market polls and focus group research, which are much more numerous than political polls contain highly proprietary information and are never released. So they are not noticed.

To some degree the findings of market research can be deduced by anyone who takes a crack at "reverse engineering" one of the zillion print ads or daily broadcast commercials, to uncover the message behind the "message from the sponsor."

It might intrigue you on a dull day to try "reverse engineering" by asking yourself what research findings led the corporate sponsor to create some ad. You'll learn that the sponsor's message inserted into your brain is not fair, balanced and truthful, but you already know that. Most market research seems so inconsequential and is so invisible to consumers that caring about the quality of the research seems irrelevant and such questioning never occurs, even by investigative media. But the very opposite can be true, as this story illustrates.

A Case History. The huge incentives for biased market research and the ease of producing erroneous findings by giant Wal-Mart Corp. illustrates how costly to the whole country advertising can be that is deceptive by omission. In a major story, *Business Week* (Oct. 6, 2003, p. 102) introduced its readers to the unique role of Wal-Mart in the economy:

"With $245 billion in 2002 revenues, Wal-Mart Stores Inc. is the world's largest company, three times the size of No. 2 retailer, France's Carrefour. Every week, 138 million shoppers visit Wal-Mart's 4,750 stores; last year, 82% of American households made at least one purchase at Wal-Mart."

Many people know that the big-box stores, like Wal-Mart, Target, and K-Mart, planted themselves along highways in lower cost, often unincorporated, jurisdictions just beyond high tax urban centers and bought the allegiance of shoppers by low-price loss leaders. Wal-Mart got far ahead of the others by two strategies:

(1) Stocking products of ever larger sectors of retailing. Wal-Mart aggregated in one giant big-box and in ever-expanding varieties: clothing, sporting goods, books, magazines, CDs, Videos, DVDs, appliances, hardware, garden, construction, electrical, electronic, optical, plumbing, machinery, food, groceries, meals, drugs and pharmaceuticals, until finally now there is little most consumers seek not offered at Wal-Mart.

(2) Convincing America that buying at Wal-Mart saves big money. From the beginning Wal-Mart pressed its suppliers even those in China to cut the cost to the consumer by re-designing products to give good value, generally downscale and not necessarily long-lived.

Whether a product has a long useful life can determine whether it's a bargain or not. Consider this example. A product is sold at a price 14% lower than a seemingly identical product and, when used, both products perform identically for three years, at which point the less expensive one dies while the more expensive one continues to perform well for another year. An economist will tell you the shorter-life product would be worth about 14% less and no bargain .

Over the years, Wal-Mart's market share grew enormously. In many high volume items and well-known brands, Wal-Mart's market share is now in the range of 20 to 30% and could reach 50% by the end of the decade.

Suppliers have learned that they could be cut out of a large part of their business if they did not meet Wal-Mart's cost-cutting demands. Suppliers have worked hard at cost cutting or were promptly dropped.

Inside a giant Wal-Mart store, as far as the eye can see are hundreds of signs proclaiming amazing will-not-be-undersold prices, etc. Can that tell us that Wal-Mart is cost-saving? Hardly.

Wal-Mart has unique challenges brought about by its increasing control of almost all retail sectors: (a) likely unavailability of labor and executives to fulfill its big expansion plans, (b) attacks by unions and local authorities for forcing downscale wages down further and destroying the livelihoods of neighborhood retail workers and owners, (c) the use of promotional prices to invade each new sector and after becoming the dominant consumer supplier in that sector, replacing the no longer needed promotional prices with profitable, higher prices, and (d) the Wal-Mart culture that limits the variety of informational, entertainment, and educational items because of rural, religious and cultural biases of most of its executive management.

The only way Wal-Mart will be able to get much closer to its goal to become the monopolistic retail supplier of nearly every product consumers require is to have proof that consumers benefit by lower prices. Two studies that Wal-Mart can now use as evidence for benefiting consumers are: (1) a UBS-Warburg, investment bank, study that showed that grocery prices are on average 14% lower where Wal-Mart competes and (2) a New England Consulting estimate that Wal-Mart saved its U.S. customers $20 billion in 2002, and almost $80 billion more from price cuts other retailers had to make to compete. The fact that this consulting company and an investment bank that stand to gain from Wal-Mart's growing success, and stand to be obliterated if their studies block Wal-Mart's march to monopoly, suggests that much bias may be found in these two examples of market research.

A complete, accurate study of Wal-Mart's on-going financial impact, requires the knowledge of every purchase of every item and its purchase price by every American minute-to-minute — clearly impossible. Useful studies can be simplified and produced, but would Wal-Mart finance such a study and accept its findings if the findings did not produce a conclusion that favors Wal-Mart? Of course not.

As long as Congress and the administration can be made to believe that Wal-Mart is saving consumers billions, the media, as exemplified by the *Business Week* article, will not challenge that conclusion, and the charge of monopoly will remain moot. No investigative media organization will touch it. This is one piece of market research that should not seem, like a print ad or a broadcast commercial, so inconsequential and so invisible to consumers that it is ignored and irrelevant. Forget *raising* the poll vaulting bar. The market research bar is so low, a limbo dancer couldn't get *under* it.

In our further description of spin, TV and print need to be considered separately.

Start with TV.
Panel shows often appear, at least nominally, fairly well balanced ideologically, but seldom balanced by gender or ethnicity. Often the ideological extremes are represented by the "two sides" of an argument. This is the first spin. Most issues have more than two sides, as we will consider in Chapter 4, p. 38, where we saw the

importance of a wide range of policy choices as a key factor in dampening the spinning of poll questions.

There is also a deficiency of "ordinary" people on a panel. In a show about prison issues or poverty how often have you seen an articulate ex-prisoner or homeless person on a panel? There are a lot of them, but their views are too far outside the *idea-bandwidth* acceptable to the mainstream – to coin a phrase in this bandwidth worshipping age.

The moderator, host, or facilitator, whatever the staff person working for the sponsor is called, has a personality and often shares the sponsor's or advertiser's bias. But often the bias comes from the fact that that nice expert from the *what'sitsname* organization was not mentioned as being a six-figure lobbyist for the trade association or union with a direct stake in the issue. Nor was it said that another panelist was a lifetime-member of a special interest organization defending the rights of horned owls, Republicans, rifle-owners or Democrats. (How is that for a balanced list?)

One simple question that would be so helpful if asked of each panelist before letting them talk, "Tell the audience, Will, (or Jill or Oscar), where you get your money from. Are you paid for being here?" The role of money not only dominates politics but media too. The responses will sometimes be a revelation to audiences.

Have you noticed that nobody is ever converted on a talk show from their original ideas to a different view of the subject? This is certainly true of the conflict-oriented shows, like CNNs "Cross-Fire", or the more polite formats that carry ideologues of opposite persuasion. How is it possible that there is no mind-change ever? Were those people born believing what they are saying on today's show? If not, why do we never catch a pundit at the precise moment of mind change?

This leads to more oddities. Since no one ever seems able to convince another, what then is the object of the "debate"? Why should anyone in the public audience ever be convinced of anything new? Has any "Talk-Back Live" host asked, "How many of you in the studio (or home) audience are considering changing your mind about this issue because of what you have heard on the show so far?" By the way that kind of question is key to what is called the debate-format question series in polling, where in Chapter 4, pp. 41-43, we will find out when and why people *do* or *do not* change their minds. The results are astoundingly revealing of what kind of pro and con arguments have or do not have an impact on the public's support for a particular policy, legislation, regulation, or government action.

In panel shows with greater civility discussants present their individual point of view. During the show, as all viewpoints emerge, none ever moves closer to the others. Politeness and civility is achieved by a friendly lead in for a new speaker that goes like this, "Tom has a point there, but what I think is ___ ", and what follows makes no point agreeing with Tom's, and neither Tom nor any of the other panelists are mentioned again by the speaker.

Bias comes mostly from omission, much more so than from what you do see or hear. Omission is the preferred means of pushing a bias because, well, because people notice omission less. It is hard to notice nothing when it is buried in a massive quantity of information. For example, those experts who weren't put on the show because their ideas are outside the narrow band of acceptable views that the mainstream tolerates for the issue, are unrecognized and unnoticed omissions.

An even more grievous form of omission has evolved out of an old tradition of dividing knowledge into disciplines: economics, sociology, business, anthropology, physics, chemistry, biology, engineering, environment, law, medicine, etc. – a very long list, now supplemented by many new disciplines: computers, telecommunications, high-tech warfare, molecular biology, genetic engineering, criminology, nanotechnology, robotics, forensics, etc., and most of these are divided into sub-disciplines, such as the 75 different branches of engineering: electrical, chemical, civil, etc. Business and political leaders turn to experts in one of these fields as problems arise.

The committees in Congress, for example, with jurisdiction for initial review of all legislative proposals, themselves share issue areas so finely divided that on any problem which has impact in more than one committee or subcommittee's area, there is competition for control between them. This usually leads to substandard legislative proposals developed without any cross-disciplinary input and all too often defective legislation. This one goes way beyond what is ordinarily considered spin too, but in fact can be considered the spin that each discipline or profession puts on its assumptions about the world.

All of this has grown slowly as knowledge has built up with the growth of research and the burgeoning of university and post-grad degree holders in the professions. As a consequence there are experts in hundreds, even thousands, of different fields and subfields whom – following in the footsteps of business, educational and political leaders – the media now use whenever an unusual, interesting news development needs that kind of expertise on the air or in a print story.

Still, when a national problem is considered as being in a specific domain, for example economics, show producers put together panels of economists, usually covering the traditional "two sides" of the issue. In today's world, the two sides are generally "conservative" and "liberal". When they are covering some subject that is pretty broad for economics, like the best form of a tax cut, the expert participants readily make statements like, "I would make a smaller cut now, about $300 billion less than the President is asking for, and shore up social security with that saving." It all makes perfect sense as long as the discussion is confined to economists and the outcome are the things that, at best, economists are knowledgeable about.

But what is omitted from the panel are experts in fields that have learned a lot, particularly in the last 30 years, about what people need and want, such as sociologists, anthropologists, psychologists, biologists, historians, ecologists, and others who might immediately be able to suggest ways that small portions of that $300 billion saving could be used that everybody – except economists – would agree are much more desirable than an economist's suggestion. "Generalists" are required who have an interest in all fields, which is precisely what the general public is. (Really? Well, think, "the total knowledge and expertise of the public" – OR – think,"all of us are smarter than any one of us".) The best that can be done by media producers, other than conducting high quality public interest polling is to represent "generalists" by experts in the complementary fields, sociologists, anthropologists, scientists, etc. This omission is very broad, goes way beyond simple spin, and is simply not recognized by panel or issue talk show producers and hosts.

Advertisers seldom place commercials on programs they perceive as unfriendly. They simply prefer not to have their commercials aired on shows that their customers are less likely tuned in to – perhaps because the show's content is unsettling or incompatible with the commercials' mood and sales theme. Then there is the distraction of 8 minutes of commercials distributed inside of and supported by 22 minutes of content in each half hour. This commercial "necessity" produces short content time segments of at most 5 or 10 minutes. What happens? Just at the most interesting moment, it's "TIME'S UP". The moderator has to sign off for the commercial.

Mainstream TV commentators and reporters are hired for their TV "presence". They are outgoing, affable, calm, clear, smiling, fast-talking and cool when forced to handle and recover from little glitches. They have the on-camera traits that TV prizes, and are not selected for deep understanding, experience or knowledge of the subjects on which the script has them speak. They are almost invariably deficient in the subject matter. (What do you expect – all of those personality traits plus a PhD in rocket science too?) They are unable to ask the hard and penetrating questions. Since this is true of all of the staff talking heads – read "wannabee stars" – behind the microphones and cameras, they never even learn that there *are* hard and unasked questions. Alternatively, there are some anti-intellectual shock jockeys who play up one-sided and shallow views on issues, serving the public no better.

Now turn to print.
Here the spin is more deliberate. Prominence in layout, placement vis-à-vis front or section lead page, titles, box sidebars, headlines, font size, and column inches, tells us which stories the publisher wants us to think are the important ones and which to ignore. "Ignore" is not a strong enough word. They are really seeking that you don't remember the item at all; don't think about it – ever again.

A recent development in mainstream newspapers and magazines follows a practice long at the heart of commercial TV. Publishers increasingly sell multi-page advertising section inserts, thought of as "news supplements" to industry groups, foreign countries, trade associations, and wealthy organizations. These inserts get attention and perhaps greater readership from the public for several reasons. They are carefully designed not to have the look and feel of traditional advertising. The ads they do carry are "newsy", built around and compatible with the content of well-written and interesting articles and editorials prepared by the insert sponsors. Major, trusted publications, including the Washington Post, TIME, Newsweek, Business Week, and others regularly run such lucrative "advertorials." In the case of public interest organization sponsors, who often favor placing full page statements in the New York Times and Washington Post covering topics like education and health care, they frequently have more salient and important information than can be found in the rest of the publication.

Sometimes a news editor wants to make a story appear inclusive and balanced that will be a public relations problem for a corporation that is a current or a future potential advertiser in the paper. The story could deservedly place the company in a bad light. The editor, working easily with layout, solves the problem by placing the story to minimize notice and impact. Perhaps in a low-circulation edition, perhaps given one-column inch in the living arts section, perhaps put on page twelve with an 8-point head, but never with a big headline on page one that the story itself justifies. Mr. Editor, are you still looking for another way to cover a story that will have absolutely zero impact? Then, just send in the boring reporter, or if the only reporter available is competent and fairly conscientious, then edit the juice out of her story and cut it down to six lines.

All of this was much easier for magazines of the 1999-2000 bubble era, the darlings Wired, Red Herring, and Upside that became so fat with advertising, stories and columns that up to six hundred page issues were the norm. Broader, capitalism-booster magazines like Fortune and the Economist can more easily bury out-of-sight undesired stories that today's capitalists prefer to ignore without gutting the story itself. Such articles primarily are about the trashing of the environment, while environmentalists viewpoints are minimized or stories about how social goods could be provided if capitalism could be reformed and updated. For example, 99% of the coverage of the expansion of wireless handheld communications devices is covered as euphoric, multi-level technical, economic and business stories, while the coverage of the public health hazards following from the proliferation of outdoor microwave radiation, cell phone towers and devices held a few inches from the brain is less than 1% of the total. The euphoric 99% makes no mention of health hazards. Few funds are available to research such health issues. They are buried and forgotten.

The most insidious and little known omission arises from the drive of on-camera TV types or hot-shot reporters, syndicated columnists, and new multi-media types who'll do anything, alright *almost* anything, to make it BIG. At the start of their careers they absorb the unwritten rules for getting ahead. No. 1 rule: handle the advertisers, potential advertisers, and officials-in-control carefully. These control-oriented folks are pretty much all affiliated or employed by large corporations and bureaucracies.

The media types learn to make few and short, preferably, "no comments" on commercials or print ads, even when occasionally they might honestly have something favorable to say. Why – if it is favorable? Because if a media type does say something favorable a couple of times, then NOT saying anything becomes a silent condemnation implying something negative is brewing. The simple rule for the media personality is "just keep away from it".

That is called *self-censorship*. And it is very effective. In totalitarian dictatorships, the most effective censorship comes from self-censorship by some 99+% of authors, editors, reporters, and anchors that just want to get ahead. All that the agents of the state have to do is to make a dramatic example of one or two that go too far over the line, perhaps by ostracism or jail-time. In the US at the start of the twenty-first century the same forces and reactions are basically present even in our democracy. No one now is shipped to the gulag. (Guantanamo, anyone?) Still criticism of owners and advertisers is muted, often non-existent because of self-censorship.

A few exceptions are allowed. One is curmudgeon Andy Rooney of CBS's "Sixty Minutes" who specializes in merciless criticism of the inconvenience and irritation visited upon all of us by the powers that be. But Andy confines his objects of scorn to readily visible lowest-common-denominator defects of products and services and to overblown marketing hype, keeps away from intellectually challenging situations, and sprinkles his comments with amusing ironic twists. Speaking his mind, he is a surrogate for the rest of us who would like to be able to give a national audience a piece of our minds too. Andy is obviously much happier after unloading and this helps fulfill his surrogate role well since we imagine that in his shoes we too would be happy. We enjoy sharing his joy. Then there are comedians, Jon Stewart and others, who in the old tradition of the jester can say the truth as long as it is mixed in with exaggeration and distortion or trashing irrelevant subjects too.

In the US, there is a ubiquitous form of spin now spreading world-wide via globalization of media: consumerism. No serious talk is permitted in or via the media on *reducing* consumption and *not* buying. This creeping, commercial self-censorship also is evident in the ownership structures that force most US media to be profit-driven. Even political candidates who used to be guaranteed free time now pay high rates to buy ads. Nowhere in TV, radio, or print media are there mentions that the Fairness Doctrine provisions of the Federal Communications Commission was lobbied off the books by the National Association of Broadcasters during the Reagan administration or that the "equal time" provision, giving political candidates free air-time access to voters, came under attack by special interests and was repealed in 1979. Today Americans seem to have forgotten that the public owns the airwaves.

When polling is not done consistently on the same basis, erroneous and confusing conclusions emerge. *Business Week* (6/24/02, 338) compared the amount of the US public's trust in corporations, in the wake of major scandals hammering US stock markets. The comparison was based on a question asked five times in the preceding 2 1/2 years. You might expect the *Business Week* surveys to show willingness to invest would drop along with trust, but they did not. In fact, when asked June 2002, for the first time a majority said their investment policies would not change.

How come? The questions were asked of investors only! Those dropping out of investments were not allowed into the survey and every one of them would say their investments had dropped, not stayed the same. If they had been included in a random sample, the balance would have slipped significantly toward decreasing willingness to invest. The sample, biased by leaving out those no longer investing, created the erroneous result. And the spin goes on.

What about facts; how do the media handle them? Facts must be treated factually with respect, unless of course a little context is used to cast doubt on their factual status. It is simple to do that. Ankara is the capital of Turkey – a fact. Want to cast doubt? Say "Ankara, the so-called capital of Turkey" or say "For some reason almost nobody knows that Ankara is the capital of Turkey" (implication: maybe it is being shifted to Istanbul). When the fact is so clearly either a fact or not, these implications are a joke, yet sometimes powerfully effective. Or an announcer says, "There was a record low temperature at International Falls yesterday" adding with a laugh "so much for global warming, ha, ha." Or a paraphrase of George W. Bush's statement to Congress about how logical (if you still believe in Skinner's failed behaviorist theories) it is to improve education by teaching how to pass tests, "If the required school tests are properly designed, they will cover just what 'we' (meaning, but not saying, 'top leaders') want students to learn. That's the definition of properly designed. Teaching students to pass the tests is exactly what good teachers will and should do. It's as simple as that.

A poll result (like "48% said "yes") is a fact, or will be presented as a fact. The statement that is made that presents the piece of poll data can always be made factual by an appropriate context, even if, and especially if, it comes from a dubious poll. It should not be presented as a fact of dubious value, which is usually the way a poll question result on its own is presented. The only way a current news-reader or pundit can present a poll result with the underlying message that "this one is to be believed" is to say that the finding has been found "by *all* the polls."

Any single poll result can be mentioned as if it were an opinion, "You have your poll result and I have mine". For pundit purposes one man's poll is as good as another's. So no poll result can be treated as being very significant. Even before any spin is considered by anybody, the question stands: is it worth trying to put spin on a baseball pitch if the ball is going to hit the ground far from the strike zone. It's a balk or a wild pitch. No spin is necessary. Spin or no spin doesn't matter. No one is paying attention.

We only get to put a spin on poll results when there is a serious effort to make the poll result widely known and high impact. That, as we shall see, happens frequently.

An example.
A public-interest polling organization (PIPA, the Program on International Policy Attitudes and the Center for International and Security Studies at the University of Maryland) in a survey "Americans on terrorism: Two Years After 9/11" asked a series of questions on the Patriot Act the same week as a Gallup poll showed **69%**

of Americans believe the USA Patriot Act is "about right" or does not go "far enough" in restricting people's civil liberties in order to fight terrorism." The question wording characterizes the Act as making it "easier for the federal government to get information on suspected terrorists through court-ordered wiretaps and searches" -- language implying that the Act's provisions are benign, fair, and routine.

The PIPA poll introduces the Patriot Act as removing "certain limitations on the government's ability to monitor and detain individuals", a fair and balanced statement with no hint of bias, unlike the Gallup introduction. The PIPA poll has these findings:

75% say "have" to the question "Is it your impression that American citizens 'have' or 'have not' been detained by the US under suspicion of being involved with a terrorist group?"

74% say yes to "If American citizens are detained by the US under suspicion of being involved with a terrorist group, is it your impression that they have the right to meet with a lawyer in their defense?"

If the preceding question is enlarged to "should have the right", support goes up to **80%**.

66% say they are somewhat or very "concerned that removing limitations on the government's ability to monitor and detain individuals may, in some cases, lead the government to go too far." This is roughly the opposite of the Gallup finding.

Gallup is a commercial pollster, aiming to please its client by finding that most people accept restricted civil liberties to fight terrorism. (A good guess is that Gallup's client is in, or a supporter of, the Bush administration.)

Another PIPA Poll Example
From the best US intelligence reports available in 2003, in Aug-Oct, PIPA determined that:
  o The Iraq-Al Qaeda Relationship before the war was slim,
  o Saddam Hussein was not involved in the Sep 11th terrorist attacks,
  o Weapons of mass destruction had not been found in Iraq during or after the war,
  o Chemical and biological weapons had not been used by Iraq in the war.

PIPA polls showed significant numbers of the public believed that US intelligence showed the opposite:
  o the Iraq-Al Qaeda relationshp was close (48%),
  o Saddam Hussein personally was likely involved in the Sep 11th attacks (69%),
  o weapons of mass destruction had been found (22%), and
  o chemical and biological weapons had been used in the war (20%),

and that these misperceptions were significantly linked to the support for starting the war and linked to where people get most of their news. Of those with one or more misperceptions, getting most of their news from Fox were 80%, CBS 71%, ABC 61%, NBC 55%, CNN 55%, print media 55%, and PBS-NPR 23%.

Why should we trust PIPA, a public-interest pollster, more than a Gallup or a Fox?

Credibility of PIPA and Public-Interest Polling

As a matter of full disclosure I must declare that I, along with four other prominent pro-bono pollsters, had a hand in designing questions for Steven Kull, the Principal Investigator for the PIPA survey. Four of Kull's highly regarded people had designed the questionnaire and wrote the analysis. The survey was funded by grants from the Rockefeller Brothers Fund and the Ford Foundation.

But there is still more to it. I am one of the 11 members of the PIPA Board of Advisors that includes my ATI (Americans Talk Issues) colleague of 16 years, Fred Steeper, Republican pollster for the two Presidents George Bush during both their campaigns and their presidencies. When Steeper polls for the President or any other Republican official, he does what commercial pollsters do. He uncovers how to present the policies, regulations, legislation, and actions that his client favors, so that the public in general and the client's constituencies in particular will be most satisfied. When he works on non-profit public-interest surveys, after sixteen years of hands-on experience, he knows the objective is to find government actions that most satisfy the general public *when the issue and polling experts designing the survey are required to seek and offer response choices from among a wide range of possibilities, representing not only Democrat and Republican favorites, but also any idea that has anything going for it. The choices must be carefully phrased to be clear, fair, accurate, and collectively balanced.*

A poll doing all of that, on almost any governance issue, uncovers entirely different public opinion than commercial pollsters find polling on the same issue. Publicly released commercial polls still far outnumber public-interest polls, so that the public seldom gets a glimpse of that great difference.

Whose findings are more reliable, a PIPA or a Gallup or Fox? Having used "fair and balanced" to describe public-interest poll questions for many years before Rupert Murdoch launched Fox News, thus putting the "fair and balanced" phrase in the public domain, I feel free to answer the question of who is more reliable with a remark borrowed from Fox News, "We report, you decide". I am fully justified in supporting the reliability and encouraging the dissemination of PIPA's findings that percentages of Fox News viewers had misperceptions on major national issues far larger than those who get most of their news from other standard sources.

A Further Example – Spin from the NY Times

We don't want to display the stupidity of just right wing and centrist media. Let's look at a good example of the backwardness and obtuseness of the *New York Times*. On 8/15/97 the lead editorial, lead sentence, of the *Times* gave credit to Bill Richardson, the United States representative at the United Nations, for a so-labled "ingenious" proposal to remedy an old UN problem, the frequent hobbling and ineffectiveness of the Security Council, the only UN entity authorized by the UN Charter to take military action. The Security Council has five permanent members that are unrepresentative of most of the world and any one of them can veto any action. The idea of increasing the number of new permanent members had been discussed within the international agencies and studied by non-governmental organizations (NGOs) for years. Richardson's ingenious proposal was to add five more permanent members. Richardson would not say whether these new members would also have the veto.

Three years earlier I and my colleagues at ATI had conducted in the U.S. many surveys on UN issues, all made available to the news media. We found that

Adding to the Security Council new permanent members "that have become important or represent larger developing nations, such as . . . . [five countries mentioned]" was favored by 80% of the public and strongly favored by 42%.

An 81% majority favored a reasonable increase in UN dues payments from new permanent members. Only 27% favored admission of new permanent members with the veto right, 65% opposed.

So the *Times* lead editorial considered a proposal ingenious that had been favored by 80% of the U.S. public three years earlier. Further, Richardson was relegated to being one among only 8% of the public who did not answer whether new permanent members should have the veto. NGOs and the U.S. people understood the value of these proposals long before the *Times* found them *ingenious*.

The editors of mainstream news media to this day have not recognized that many of the civil society organizations, the NGOs that represent the people, are out in front in understanding where the world is and should be going. Did the U.S. pay a price for the obtuseness of the mainstream media? Yes, it did. The people were not informed of increasing Soviet weakness and the rise of civil society there and in

Eastern Europe and South Africa from 1980 onward. The ending of the Cold War to the vast majority of the people (who only heard or saw mainstream news) appeared to happen mysteriously during 1989.

Perpetual Spinning of the Most Important News by Mainstream Media

Does the obtuseness still go on? Yes it does. Considering problems produced by "rogue dictators" the mainstream news media and special interest pollsters see solutions one of two ways, either diplomatic efforts or military intervention. Little else gets serious consideration. The efforts of NGOs seems beyond the ability of media to handle. Perhaps, as explained by Hazel Henderson in "Building a Win-Win World" (1996), slow motion good news does not fit into a news media treatable category. As a result, NGO efforts, seldom noticed by the media, are little understood by the public. Remarkably, this is independently confirmed by a poll question asked just after the revolutions of 1989, by Market Strategies Inc, pollsters for Pres. George Bush, Sr.: "Some people have commented that in places like Eastern Europe and South Africa the people WITHOUT the guns are winning. Can you understand what they mean by that?" Yes, 53% No, 44%.

The U.S. public was so kept in the dark by mainstream media that almost half did not even understand the question. But look what happened when the follow-up question was asked of the majority that said "Yes":

"Do you agree or disagree with the comment that the people WITHOUT the guns are winning?" A whopping 82% agreed. Media moguls, anchors, editors, and reporters don't understand things that the public does.

We are paying the price for it again. George W. Bush agreed on 9/9/02 to some diplomatic initiatives before the U.S. intervenes militarily in Iraq (with 68% of U.S. public approval). The mainstream U.S. media still has not tried to make clear why and how the people without the guns can and do win. So it is likely that again it will be "off to war we go."

o oo ooo oooo ooooo oooo ooo oo o

Note: Much of this chapter was developed from personal interviews with futurist Hazel Henderson, a long-time media analyst (see her Building a Win-Win World, Chapter 5, "Government by Mediocracy" (1996)

Chapter 4. The 21st Century Issues – Globalization, Terrorism, Outsourcing/Immigration, and the Quality of Life

Introducing Globalization

Little attention was paid to the centuries-long process that in the early 1990's was finally labeled "globalization." Observers are realizing that resolving issues raised by globalization will be a dominant feature of world affairs– and, more than that, a titanic struggle – for the rest of the 21st century. The broad range of expert opinions implies that no outcome – for better or worse – can be ruled out.

This chapter will present survey research findings starting from the early part of the 1990s decade showing that people, collectively, have been ahead of leaders in understanding the many aspects of globalization, when presented to them in a fair, balanced, and accurate manner. People are ready to deal with the issues raised by globalization positively and realistically. They consistently choose a direction different from what leaders have chosen, while leaders refuse to seriously address the people's preferences.

Dealing with Globalization

Beginning over twelve years ago, ATI started asking questions about globalization. In 1991 one set of questions dealt with the many different aspects of the subject:

#1. Designing, manufacturing, and marketing a global product in many countries;
#2. Instant 24-hour trading of stocks, bonds, and currencies around the world;
#3. Multinationals manufacturing in countries with cheap labor and weak environmental laws;
#4. Workers all over the world going to other countries to work;
#5. Pollution crossing international borders;
#6. Global arms sales and arming of third world countries;
#7. Global news, advertising, entertainment, and information programs and software.

People were asked whether (a) the US should seek international agreements for regulating these activities as opposed to (b) not seeking such agreements or the US regulating them. The findings (ATI-17, Q17-23) were in **rank order:**

Percent of public support for US to seek international regulatory agreements:

#5. pollution	90%	#1. global products	64%
#6. arms sales	85%	#4. workers far from home	62%
#3. manufacturing globally	73%	#7. information circulating globally	34%
#2. securities trading	66%		

Note that pollution, the only activity among all aspects of globalization that no country by itself can stop from entering its borders, receives the most support for regulation. An overwhelming majority of 90% supports regulating pollution. The only regulation that can stop pollution from entering any country that wants to stop it is *international* regulation. Multinational corporations, heavily advertising in the mainstream media, have worked relentlessly in the last ten years in the opposite direction, trying, in the name of the "free market", to deregulate globalization. Attention to pollution works against the corporations' free market mantra, so they avoid mentioning global pollution.

In more recent years the mainstream news media began speaking of globalization as if the word meant only economic globalization – international free markets. So coming into awareness of the situation years after the "average, ordinary" person was able to readily consider how to deal with globalization, the mainstream media "misunderstood" the totality of aspects of globalization and, together with politicians and corporations, added to the confusion. The "ordinary" person was, and still is, ahead of its leaders in business, the media, and government.

Notice that #7 is the only aspect of globalization that a majority does not favor regulating. This is not surprising because of American's strong support for free speech and "information wants to be free." In the seven aspects of globalization, the DKs ranged from 4% to 11%, none large enough to affect any of these conclusions.

The polls showed that the well-educated were more favorable and familiar with these aspects of globalization and more aware of their opportunities. Data below illustrates how the less-well-educated knew back then that they would be more vulnerable. They were proved right by many studies in the following years. These have shown the uneven impacts of globalization on the poor, the uneducated, or those in regions bypassed by global financial and electronic networks.

Since then US opinion favoring regulation of globalization has been forced into mass movements, such as the many thousands whose leaders attended the Porto Alegre, Brasil, World Social Forums in 2001 and 2002.

Our leaders still do not have a clue as to how to handle economic globalization in a satisfactory way. In contrast, when presented with adequate choices the "ordinary" people pick the one that could make economic globalization work by understanding and caring for the needs of real people living in the real world, pollution and all.

Early Trend in Non-Support Continues into the 21ˢᵗ Century
Questions on support for globalization asked in Nov '91 and March '93 were based on this definition of globalization:

Many business transactions and other activities, which used to take place between people and groups within a country, are NOW taking place more frequently, and on a GLOBAL scale, between people and groups across many different countries. This change has been called 'globalization.'

Do you think this is a generally POSITIVE development in the world, a NEGATIVE development, or are you NOT FAMILIAR with this idea of 'globalization?'" (PROBE: "Would that be VERY or SOMEWHAT?")

Here we use the convention that instructions to interviewers are given in caps and interviewers must make sure that words in caps are heard by the respondent R Responses:

	ATI #21 March '93	Total	ATI #17 Nov. '91
Very positive	18%	} 41%	46%
Somewhat positive	23%		
Somewhat negative	7%	} 14%	9%
Very negative	7%		
Not familiar	43%		42%
Don't Know	2%		3%
Total DK		45%	45%

Notice how many accept the "Not familiar" choice. Including the small "Don't Know"s almost half of the people, and the same percentage, 45%, both in '91 and in '93 are quite willing to opt out of making a substantive choice in this question. Those who do make a substantive choice shifted significantly to being negative about globalization even in these early months of globalization, long before any political leader had ever mentioned globalization. The people were beginning to see where our leaders were trying to take us. There was a strong educational dependence on welcoming globalization even in 1991. Of those with post-graduate degrees, 82% were familiar with globalization, 77% believed it a positive development and 74% believed the world was moving in the right direction. In contrast, for those with high-school or less, the figures were respectively, 42%, 38%, and 32%.

People's Preferred Approach to Resolving Globalization Issues

Long before the street theater demonstrations started at World Trade Organization (WTO) meetings in Seattle and Prague in 2000, and long before the demonstrations protesting government leaders meeting in Quebec in 2001 to expand the trade and tariff provisions of the North American Free Trade Agreement (NAFTA) to include Central and South America, ATI asked a number of related questions in a 1993 survey.

After a warm-up question on a regional trade agreement, NAFTA, linking Canada and Mexico with the US, and a global free trade agreement, the General Agreement on Trade Tariffs (predecessor of the WTO), ATI asked two questions, **Q6, Q6a**, about support for a solution to the problem of globalization, with this preamble:

"Whether we go for global or regional trade agreements, these agreements are crafted by economists who focus on economic aspects. The economists get VERY LITTLE input from other scientific advisors, like anthropologists, social scientists, and ecologists who often do see ways to protect a country's social institutions, culture, economy, and environment."

Q6. Do you think that experts in other social and physical sciences should be involved in the development of trade agreements, or should the agreements be designed by economists alone, and not be complicated by competing viewpoints?

Other experts should be involved	71%	Neither (volunteered)*	1%
Economists should design agreements alone	23%	DK (volunteered)*	5%

* significance of "volunteered" responses in next chapter

Q6a. Let's go into that a little bit more. There are two points of view on this issue: (ROTATE)

Here is the first one: some people say that a combination of economists and experts from social and physical sciences would produce trade agreements more acceptable to everyone. The amount of time spent as these professionals learn to work together would be wisely invested, as they are sure to be more successful than the current system of economists working alone. Reaching agreements using only the limited ideas of economists will mean continuing delays in treaty approval, as well as harmful social and environmental impacts.   *65% agree.*

Here's the second one: Other people say introducing non-economic considerations will make these already complicated negotiations hopelessly more complicated, so that no agreements will be reached for an even longer time than it would take for the economists to put together satisfactory agreements. With every year that it takes to reach satisfactory agreements, each country's economy will suffer from the lost opportunities for expanded trade, jobs, and a better material standard of living.   *26% agree*

Neither...2%   In between...1%   Both...1% (volunteered)   DK...6%.

It is worth noting that Hazel Henderson, the noted futurist and author of many books on economics and international issues, developed the first point of view in **6a** and Fred Steeper, pollster for the successful campaigns for President of both Bush the elder and the younger, developed the second point of view. Both were approved by the ATI design teams of polling and issue experts as fair, balanced, accurate and strong presentations of the principal contrasting viewpoints.

The persistence of support for multiple experts, when the issue is taken up again in Q6a with much more detail than when first raised in Q6, confirms that the public's opinion holds up well when challenged on this question. Over three-to-one favor multiple experts in Q6 and it is still five-to-two in Q6a. That is impressive internal consistency. Further evidence comes from considering the substantial number of difficult questions that the public has handled in all ATI surveys and how, by every measure, findings are internally consistent. The validity of responses was further confirmed by interview monitoring and by interviewer reports that respondents' attitudes were typically thoughtful and measured, as well as by later events, such as the '97 defeat in Congress of "fast track" trade agreements, which ignore broader issues.

In fields where the establishment – the universities, foundations, government, media, and industry – engages or uses large numbers of diverse experts, most experts never address questions like Q6 and Q6a. The framing of such questions challenges their own assumptions about how experts should be used in the political process. Experts stay away from challenging the expertise of highly credentialed experts in any field, not just their own field. You might call this practice "professional courtesy." Other experts are reluctant to challenge economists on their own turf, trade issues, even by arguing that experts from other social sciences should be heard. Experts find it hard to answer questions like Q6 and Q6a.

People in general do not find it hard. People are less impressed by *expertise.* They have noticed that, in the case at hand, economists seem to have no better record than random walkers throwing darts at a dart board in prescribing for economies, fixing them, or predicting future economic performance. By '96, elite opinion had moved closer to the public view, with such expert agencies as the World Bank conceding that economists needed inputs from social and environmental scientists in devising their development and trade policies.

But the struggles between elites and the people on all issues that will likely dominate the 21st century, globalization, terrorism, immigration/outsourcing, and quality-of-life, are in 2004 still at an early stage. After a brief discussion of a very valuable technique in good polling, the *battery*, illustrated in the first set of questions in this chapter (ATI#17, Q17-23) we will return to quality-of-life-indicators, one of the major issues, beyond globalization, likely to dominate the world in the 21st century. Two fascinating questions on terrorism appeared in Chapter 3, pp. 29-31. A full range of immigration and outsourcing issues, barely touched here under globalization, will emerge in the years ahead.

The *Battery* – Multiple Choices in the Same Frame – a Boon for Good Polling

The first set of questions in this chapter asked about regulating seven items, the various aspects of globalization. The frame or pre-amble that introduces the seven items contains all aspects that the items have in common. If only two items, it's a *binary* question. With more than two it's a *battery*. The persistence of the public's response choices over time is amazingly stable, changing not at all or slowly over the years *unless* a major event occurs that is relevant to the question and then if there is a significant change, it is usually in the expected direction and in the same direction for all major demographic sectors of the public.

The rank order of the battery items also is very persistent, in the sense that if the question is repeated in later surveys with new items added to the battery or old deleted, then those items that are the same in both the earlier and later survey generally rank in the same order, or close thereto.

A single battery is the only fair way to compare like things. Voting in a democratic election is a form of polling. For each office to be filled, the public is asked to make its choice, from among all candidates on the ballot. The most votes elects. As in polling, all the candidates must be offered in a single battery, to accurately reflect the preferences of the voters. The 2003 California recall election, with a ballot in two parts, elected Schwarzenegger governor by the rules established by the California courts for that election, which prohibited recounts. However, the outcome did not reflect the public's preference, which is the democratic standard in US elections, even during recounts in the flawed FL 2000 national election. (See Chapter 13, pp. 119-123.)

The Debate Format

When we have already determined the public's support for a policy, if we then present the public with pro and con arguments for and against the policy, after the arguments are completed we re-ask the original question to determine how well the original support held up. When the question asked of each argument is, "How *convincing* is" or "Were you *aware* of" this argument?, a three point non-numerical scale, such as: (1) very, (2) somewhat, or (3) not at all, *convincing* or *aware* gives the data needed. The sequential set of questions are: (a) policy, first asking (b) pro and con arguments, (c) policy, second asking. This question-set constitutes a *debate format*.

ATI#24 was largely devoted to using this extremely valuable technique to test public opinion on support for four specific proposals for improving Congress: term limits, campaign funding to limit contributions from outside a members district, a Congressional Office of Public Opinion Research and Assessment (COPORA), and the establishment of Quality-of-Life (QOL) Indicators.

ATI has tested many variations of the debate format, both using different samples and within the same samples. Variations of debate-format question-sets have been used to study:

o The effect of omitting the first asking, [(a) above],
o The effects of relative placements of pro and con arguments
o The relationships between the changing of support for the proposals and the relative strength of pro and con arguments in being convincing or aware, both "strongly" and "somewhat",
o The effects of wording changes on findings (e.g. in the arguments using "convincing" or "aware"),
o The effect of asking only pro arguments, or only con arguments, to determine how much the public's position can be moved by one-sided arguments.
o The effect of different scales (Scale effects examined in Chapter 8, pp. 69-72)
and others

Findings have shown internal consistency and reasonableness. An example of a debate format question-set is given in **One-Sided Arguments** at the end of this chapter. The public digs in its heels largely resisting being pushed in one direction.

A most unexpected finding from debate formats used both in ATI#24 and in other surveys, was that the changes in support from before to after the "debate" showed little net variations. There was indeed typically a much larger fraction of respondents who, based on hearing the arguments, switched both to and from supporting the proposal, but in such a way that largely cancelled each other out, leaving a much smaller net change. This led to a new theory of how the public changes its mind, called the *dynamic equilibrium* of public opinion. (See *Locating Consensus for Democracy*, p. 308)

Quality-of-Life (QOL) Indicators – Illustrating the Debate Format

Hazel Henderson pioneered critiques of the GNP as the overall scorecard of progress. She contended that per capita GNP growth conceals other concerns such as whether the poverty gap is widening or to what extent economic growth causes hidden environmental and social costs, while ignoring "subsidies" of unpaid housework, parenting, and volunteering. (See Paradigms in Progress (1991); Beyond Globalization (1999) and Henderson's other books at www.hazelhenderson.com) Henderson created with the Calvert group of socially responsible mutual funds the Calvert-Henderson Quality of Life Indicators (updated regularly at www.Calvert-Henderson.com).

The proposal for quality-of-life indicators has become increasingly more widely known around the world, but still obscure in the US. Globally accepted indicators of QOL will become a contentious issue for the 21st century. QOL is part of the slow-motion good news that the mainstream news media do not cover well. Organizations for environmental and consumer protection, corporate and government accountability, and human rights took up the demand for better indicators of real wealth and progress.

The ATI team, including Henderson, formulated the QOL proposal initially for ATI#22, where it was found to be in great favor with the public. It was time that it, too, be subjected to the debate format. It was retested in ATI#24 in part, as an experiment to pro-actively test public opinion on a reform which cuts across all issues – since neither political party nor pundits had suggested broadening GNP or including additional scorecards in other major areas of concern to voters.
In its first asking (See Table 6) this QOL proposal became the top scoring, (81%) among all 50 proposals for government reform tested in ATI#22 and #24. In its second asking, support dropped slightly. Any proposal that scores at 81% favorable in its first asking is so high to begin with that to stay that high after the arguments were heard, the pro arguments would have to have been almost five times more likely to move a neutral or opposed respondent up to favoring it than to move a respondent favoring it down to neutral or opposed. Dropping to 76% meant that it was only four times as likely. For this proposal, only two pro and two con

Table 6. Quality of Life Indicators

Do you favor this proposal: % favor

1. In the same way we've developed and use the Gross National Product to measure the growth of the economy, this proposal would develop and use a scorecard of new indicators for holding politicians responsible for progress toward OTHER national goals, like improving education, extending health care, preserving the environment, and making the military meet today's needs.   **81%**

Tell me if you think these arguments for and against term limits are VERY, MODERATELY, A LITTLE, OR NOT AT ALL convincing.

                                                                  very convincing

2. President Clinton has ordered the revision of the economic indicator, the Gross National Product, or GNP, so that it will conform to international standards. However, full scorecards of indicators of progress are now being developed in many nations. Supporters say we must expand our scorecards to cover quality-of-life indicators in all areas so we can hold our politicians accountable for their campaign promises as well as to compare our performance with that of other nations.   **43%**

3. Opponents say that eventually economists will be able to calculate a single indicator of progress, a kind of enlarged GNP, that bundles into this money-based statistic our progress in all major areas including the economy, health, education, the environment, and so forth. This single number would be easier for everyone to use to rank ourselves against other nations and to judge the performance of our political leaders.   **22%**

4. Supporters think that economists weighing all these quality-of-life indicators in money terms and bundling them up into the GNP will produce an index that almost no one will understand. They say we should develop scorecards that use data already available to map specific progress in all major areas. This is less costly, more informative, and could be in use very soon.   **40%**

5. Opponents say the main indicator of progress for a long time has been the GNP which gives the economic progress of the whole country. The most objective way we have to track the progress of the country is in money terms. Other social and environmental statistics won't be as objective and will just be used by various groups like the environmentalists and the education lobby, to push their pet causes.   **22%**

                                                                       % favor

6. Now that you have considered all these arguments, rate the original proposal again.   **79%**

7. Do you favor or oppose this proposal?   **76%**

arguments were thought necessary. The pro arguments were considered very convincing by almost twice as many respondents as the con arguments. Since the nature of the con arguments was that they addressed the pro arguments (and vice versa), rather than the proposal, instead of keeping pro and con separate and rotating them as groups, in this case ATI alternated them.

One-Sided Arguments
The structure of the debate format in ATI #2, Q51 through Q56 was somewhat different from the standard question-set sequence. Its sequence was: policy, policy variation, two con arguments, policy. It shows that the public's position differs completely from what is supported by the leaders and the major news media and is not much moved by the opposing arguments:

ATI #2, Dec. '87, Q51. As a general goal, which of these two do you think is more desirable:

The elimination of all nuclear arms in the world	56%
For a few major countries including the US to have enough nuclear arms so no country would dare attack them	41%
DK	3%

Q52. *If "elimination of all nuclear arms in the world," ask:* What is the lowest reduction in nuclear arms in the world over the next few years that you would consider satisfactory – reduced by 20%, 50%, 90%, or eliminated completely:

Reduced by 20%	11%
Reduced by 50%	27%
Reduced by 90%	10%
Eliminated completely	51%
DK	2%

Q53/54. Some people say that nuclear weapons actually have helped prevent war and the world would be more dangerous without them. Have you heard this opinion before?

Yes...71%   No...28%   DK...4%

Q55. What these people point out is that the United States and the Soviet Union do not dare start a war with each other because each side would be destroyed by the other side's nuclear weapons. If they eliminated all their nuclear weapons, they would be more likely to go to war. What is your opinion – do you think eliminating all nuclear weapons would make war between the United States and the Soviet Union more likely, less likely, or wouldn't make a difference?

More likely	27%
Wouldn't make a difference	47%
Less likely	22%
DK	4%

Q56. In view of what we just spoke of, I'd like to know if your opinion to an earlier question has changed or stayed the same. The question is: As a general goal, which of these two do you think is more desirable:

The elimination of all nuclear arms in the world	53%
For a few major countries including the US to have enough nuclear arms so no country would dare attack them	43%
Don't know/Refused	4%

This is a variation of the debate format where those favoring the policy of complete elimination initially are asked to clarify their position in Q52 and then, in two questions, all respondents are asked to evaluate a major argument against the policy, before they are asked the policy question the second time. The con argument in Q55, which impresses only about a quarter of the sample, produces a tiny change of 3 points when the basic policy question is re-asked. The public is pretty firm in this judgment. The fact that respondents, when asked about serious, sensible policy, seldom change their minds (on a net basis) is a characteristic of many issues, which we will consider more later.

Chapter 5. Three Easy Ways to Spot Spin

A little explanation of how polling works will lead us into easy ways to spot spin. Regardless of the question, some people will give a "non-substantive" answer, called a "DK" in Chapter 2, p. 14. They may say, "I'm not sure", " I dunno", "That's a tough question", "What", "I can't answer that" (surprisingly rare), and maybe they will say nothing at all – for a long time. After all, if the interview is in a shopping mall, they might turn away to chat with a passing friend, or at home they might have laid the phone down to let someone in, stop the dog from chewing up the curtains, take Johnny to the bathroom, etc. All of these non-substantive responses are dumped into the DK bin and called the DKs.

DKs can vary all over the place, from less than 1% to well over 50%. That broad range turns out to be a clue for spotting spin.
Small DKs are associated with a well-designed question that:
1. is clear, unambiguous, tightly phrased in standard language with no unnecessary words.
2. offers a range of response choices sufficiently wide so that people find one that they have no difficulty in agreeing to.
3. follows closely, naturally and logically from preceding questions in the poll or from a short preamble that serves as a stage-setting introduction.
4. people feel is important.
5. has a lot of meaning and significance. Most people know it is pertinent to things that affect their lives deeply and significantly.

A question scoring high on all of these counts will have *less than 2% DKs*.

An important kind of question, easily meeting criteria 4 and 5, is a question on what people want for governance – policy, legislation, regulation, and government actions.

In contrast, questions that typically have high DKs, usually 10% to over 50%, ask
for: o opinions on a breaking news story, or
          o an evaluation of a one time situation or an event, or
          o a prediction of what will be the outcome of event or a policy, or
          o on a subject that a significant fraction of the populace are unaware of
          o factual knowledge (like quiz show questions) and/or
are unclear, ambiguous, confusing. (Most people will not approve what they do not understand.)

Statistical analysts and academic pollsters shun criteria like these that do not lend themselves to mathematical precision. As I write, there are PhD political scientists trying to show that there is a correlation between length -- the number of words in a question – and the size of the DKs. That these two correlate is not an unreasonable conjecture. If one has never paid much attention to poll question responses, it is easy to imagine that respondents fatigued from hearing a lengthy question get confused and opt for a DK. However, the reality is that all of the above criteria, which came from the careful study of tens of thousands of question responses, show that the length of a question that has few DKs must generally be quite long – *not* short (see Chapter 9, pp. 84-89). Readers who have followed this presentation, now know an important thing about polling that many academic pollsters, who have to do fancy statistical analyses for their theses, simply do not know. Since we are only on the second page of this chapter, that's not a bad record of accomplishment. You get a good grade.

But now its time to move on and link the size of the DKs to spin. When you hear or read a poll result reported by the media, the DKs are usually not mentioned at all. Let's look at a typical example. Assume that the substantive responses actually asked in the poll were the four choices: "strongly agree", "somewhat agree", "somewhat disagree", and" strongly disagree". The media usually collapse them, by combining the two agrees and the two disagrees to get, for example: 25% agree and 65% disagree. The missing part 10% is the size of the DKs. It is the shortfall of 25 plus 65 from 100. As we said before, it's like making change. 25 + 65 + 10 pennies give you a dollar.

So if a poll result comes from the media and doesn't add up to 100%, just count the pennies, see how you are being short-changed, and estimate the size of the DKs. An added simplification is that you don't have to get the arithmetic exactly right. Because of the sampling error, you can be off by a few pennies because none of these numbers are exact.

Sometimes the media skirt DKs altogether by reporting a result this way "A new poll shows that the American people approve of school vouchers by 3 to 2." You cannot figure the DKs from that. To show the significance of this tricky way of reporting, consider two possibilities: (1) DK is 10% and (2) DK is 50%. The numbers for the 3 to 2 split then become: with (1) favor 54% and opposed 36%; and with (2) favor 30% and opposed 20%. Quite a difference! In one case a majority is in favor and in the other not even $1/3^{rd}$ of the public is in favor. Similar results will happen for other splits than 3 to 2. We cannot tell what the situation is without more information. On a school voucher question, for example, would the DKs be as large as 50%? Ah there's the rub. It may well depend on the exact wording of the question and the media seldom show us the complete question. When many people are very unfamiliar with a new subject, as globalization was over ten years ago, there can be remarkably high DKs , such as the 45% DKs on page 35, Chapter 4.

If the media does not give the percentages favoring and opposed, it is telling the public very little. Is that spin? Since most people do not even notice the DKs and don't miss them when not given (spin by "omission"), there is a widespread presumption that DKs are unimportant. Yes a small DK, is not very important. But when omitted, its size is unknown and since it still can be large, not knowing is unfair and misleading. I call that spin. It is often not the reporter who is at fault. It could be the editor, the station owner, a pr flack, or the pollster. But someone has put a spin on it. Don't trust a poll result that does not give the substantive percentages or give DK explicitly.

The DK bin acts like a safety valve. If there are no other clues that the public does not like any of the choices offered very much or cannot deal with the question itself a large DK is the best clue that spin is present.

Good pollsters often give the public other opportunities to opt out of the choices presented. They allow volunteered responses. What that means may not seem obvious until you think about the way surveys are taken. Data entry is always into a computerized system like CATI (Computer Assisted Telephone Interviews) or by hand on a pre-printed paper form. For in-person or field interviews, there are software systems functionally equivalent to CATI. This recording process is essential for quality control to make certain that all interviewers read the same questions and offer the same choices, especially in highly interactive questionnaires, where answers to one question change what the following questions will be. Only good software makes highly interactive polls practical.

We saw in Chapter 2, p. 15, that many CATI-based polls are set up to accept only choice A, choice B, and DK. No other responses are recorded and so if the respondent R responds with any substantive response except A or B, that volunteered response cannot appear in the poll data. The question in the following example in contrast allows the volunteered response into the poll data and does so by asking two different samples of the public, each sample asked in two slightly different but important ways. For one sample, volunteered response possibilities were not mentioned by the interviewer and for the other they were. When that is done here is how it works out:

Whatever number do volunteer there are also a large number who would make that same choice but only if the choice were explicitly read by the interviewer in the same way as all the other choices. Why is that? A lot of people are not pro-active. The interview may remind them of school tests or job application interviews. To pass the test or get the job, they learned not to question the questioners, to choose only from what they were offered. For long after, such people are not likely to rock the boat. Case in point. Almost everyone drafted into the army in WWII learned quickly, "Never volunteer." Here is a real question example:

Question (ATI#5, '88): In combating the drug problem, which do you think our government should concentrate MORE on: (ROTATE choices)

	Volunteered	
	NOT Mentioned	Mentioned
Stopping Americans from USING illegal drugs?:	39%	30%
Stopping other countries from PRODUCING illegal drugs?	33%	27%
Both equally (volunteered)? -- NOT Mentioned and Mentioned	24%	36%
Neither (volunteered)? – NOT Mentioned and Mentioned	3%	5%
DK	2%	2%

Note that, compared to the results in the "Mentioned" column, when the interviewer did Not mention that "Both" and "Neither" were acceptable answers, fewer responded with those choices and hence more responded with the two substantive choices. (Both columns have to add to approximately 100, including the DKs, which are negligible in this example. Yes, the first column adds to 101, due to round off error.)

Allowing all reasonable choices to be heard can be extremely important. In this example, when the volunteered was mentioned, the third place choice at 24% shot up 36% to the top of the four choices, a 50% increase.

Here is the lesson for spin spotters, if a poll result is presented by the media with some volunteered choices allowed, first be pleased that this is a fair and well-designed question – compared to those where "voluntecred" is locked out – and then, more important, recognize that the size of the sample choosing that volunteered choice would have been much larger if it had been an offered choice. "Volunteered" can be even more of a safety valve than DK, but the cases where the absence of volunteered choices can be used as a sign of spin are less frequent.

In Chapter 2 we considered the simplest question, the "binary" or "either-or" question, with two substantive answers, A and B. There is something that seems simpler than the either-or question, but in reality seldom is. That is an `A or Not-A' question". You know, "Just tell me whether you favor A or not!" This kind of a question is inherently unfair. It is kind of like a fork in the road with only one branch in the fork – the A branch. There is no other. You are being asked to either take A or what? Stop dead, I suppose.

Politicians do this all the time. They favor a proposal and state conclusively -- in a heartfelt positive way, "This great nation has no other choice." Sometimes they say this after making the case for the proposal. Sometimes out-of-the-blue. But, for all practical purposes there is always at least one other choice, often many others. Politicians want you to think that the policy choice that they and their sponsors want is "the only choice." Margaret Thatcher, former Prime Minister of the UK, by the time she had been driven from office, had such a reputation for labeling her major proposals with, "There Is No Alternative!" that her opponents in the public began to reply, "Not TINA again! There *are* better choices."

Now we have to be fair to politicians and explain that the better ones do sincerely believe TINA, "There Is No Alternative!" Here is their rationale. Throughout their political lives, they have sought the solution to a political problem with the least possible change from something that has worked before. That approach is the easiest to explain, understand and get supported. Successful politicians can make their solutions appear to work well enough that their careers are not hurt at least in the near term. But the truth is "There Is An Alternative!" Often there are many simple alternatives that would work better than what a particular politician claims is without alternative. But even when this is not the case, there is an alternative, and those who work closely with Heads-of-State know it. When within earshot of an intimate audience *not* including the Head-of-State, they relax and sometimes succumb to this moment of truth: "Heads of State always do the right thing – after all else fails."

Several, even many, "last resort" alternatives can be explored by using what is called the Systems approach. Instead of trying to affect their constituents, or indeed the whole world, in the smallest possible way, problem solvers should consider embedding their problem in a larger context, to consider the System in which the problem occurred. For example, there are hundreds of different ways of reducing hunger by directly supplying people with more food or educating them about how to get more, become a more successful beggar, obtain microcredit, etc. But the problem could be considered embedded in the larger problem of poverty. If poverty, or some aspects of poverty, could be properly tackled it might be easier to reduce hunger than by doing so directly and may improve things in many other ways too. Since people without money are considered poor, the problem of poverty is thereby embedded in the money system, which in turn is embedded in the financial system. In principle a better overall solution may be found in tackling one of the larger systems. The example illustrates that there is always an embedded nest of systems that could be tackled to solve the problem in the smallest system. In truth, it is not clear in advance how large a system is the appropriate level to look into to fix the problem. The larger the system considered, the more complex it is and the more possibilities for failure. The Systems approach should be looked into just when all politicians are screaming TINA at us. Then we gain more confidence that a larger system needs to be looked into in order to have some hope of making real progress.

"There is no other choice" is reminiscent of the "*choiceless* choice" made famous by Nazi bullyboys, who sometimes formed two lines for concentration camp inmates and allowed each person to choose to wait in one. Then both lines were led into the gas chambers by different entrances. Everybody died. Adolescent Nazi's could imagine the victims blaming themselves, just as the gas ovens were turned on, "If only I had chosen the other line." In reality, from previous experiences most Nazis, and their victims too, knew from the beginning that it was to be a *choiceless* choice.

Pollsters hired by, or otherwise favoring, a candidate for political office, know somewhat more sophisticated ways of offering *choiceless* choices. Assume the pollster wants the public to choose A. He can set up B to be close to "not-A".and build up the desirability of A by stressing its strong points. Then B, appearing to be essentially not-A, seems weak without the pollster having to say or imply any weakness in B. Alternatively if B is quite different from not-A, the pollster can describe B as a weak and inadequate proposal. Most respondents will then still choose A over B. To use more subtlety the bias in B can be made slightly negative, and the pollster may still get the result he seeks. When a bad poll question does favor A over B, while the public itself favors B, people, surprisingly often, dig in their heels and the majority will still express its preference for B. An example, **"One-Sided Arguments"**, appeared in Chapter 4, p. 42.

Public interest polling resolves this difficulty in a clean way. We use a small balanced team of polling and issue experts who design the poll, with at least one team member favoring each of the choices, in this case A and B. Before the final acceptance of wording, the whole team has to agree that the wording of the descriptions of A and of B are both as strong as they can be made without bias. If there is any question about this, then several versions of A and of B are tested in different surveys (with different samples) until this point is absolutely clear. (And the same is true for C, etc, when there are three or more substantive choices offered).

But typically commercial pollsters are willing to go with the strong version of A and the weak version of B. This puts spin on the outcome. How can you spot it? Common sense helps. Does the description of A have positive sounding phrases or of B weak, dubious, or confusing phrases? Sometimes the spin can be spotted because the A choice simply has many more words in it than the B choice.

Before leaving this subject there is one more thing that we have to say about DKs. Remember when the respondent was not responding at all to a pollster's question. Well re-asking the question still may not produce a substantive answer. There is one thing that is a no-no for the pollster, that is to say something that suggests a specific substantive answer, anything other than re-reading the entire question with all the allowed choices given equal weight and emphasis. It would be totally unprofessional and out-of-bounds for the pollster to suggest or imply that a particular substantive answer is preferred. Still, there may be more that the pollster can do that will make a difference.

Years ago, I had sent one survey to a field house and a second survey to a different field house at about the same time. Although they were designed for different purposes and had many different questions, both surveys had some important identical questions, a few with a large number of choices offered.

I was quite upset when I saw the results. For questions with the same wording in the two surveys differed by as much as 10%. I queried the two field houses and learned that the difference arose because one used a procedure called "probing the DKs" and got DKs down to about 2 or 3%, depending on the question, and the other one did not. I was relieved when I discovered that if I imagined that the percentage of extra DKs from a question in the unprobed survey were distributed to all the substantive choices, it was possible to allocate the distribution so that, post-allocation, the responses of the same question in the two surveys were in agreement with each other, often within ± 1%. Moreover, this procedure of allocating the DKs worked for all the questions that were identical in both surveys. For example, if the original results for a question asked identically in both surveys -- with the same five substantive choices offered in each, was:

Unprobed Survey: DK=11%, A=36%, B=27%, C=16%, D=6%, E=4%
Probed Survey: DK= 2%, A=40%, B=30%, C=19%, D=6%, E=4%
  Differences   9%   −4%   −3%   −3%   0   0.

The response to all of the five substantive questions in the two surveys, for example, can be made identical if we reduce the unprobed survey DK to 1%. The DKs of the two surveys differ by 1% and all other response differences are zero.

A shift of response of 10% or more is much greater than the error due to sample size, less than ±3% but it is only mentioned by pollsters when dealing with a customer who knows about this problem. The pollster can ask, "Do you want to probe the DKs?" and do whatever the customer wants. But time is money. Pollsters do not do this unless the customer really wants and will pay for it.

Allocating the DKs is not a very accurate rule-of-thumb but it can tell us something important in some cases that could not be found any other way. A remarkable study using data current on Nov 11, 2002, gives us an example that depends on the responses to just one question, the most frequently asked question in polling, a question that many different field houses ask frequently:

"Do you approve or disapprove of the way George W. Bush is handling his job as president?"

Table 1 shows the field dates of the most recent asking of this single question, by eleven different highly regarded and prominent polling organizations in the US, followed by the number of times they have each asked this question in the past 22 months (311 times altogether). The organizations are often a collaboration of three: pollster/ print news/ TV news. The field house used may or may not be independent of the collaboration.

Table 1 . In order of most recent asking (Pollsters/Print news/TV news)	most recent field dates	# of times asked this same question in past 22 months
1. Gallup/USA Today/CNN	11/8-10	68
2. PrincetonSRA/Newsweek	11/7-8	32
3. NYT/CBS News	11/2-4	33
4. Wash.Post/ABC News	10/31-11/2	26
5. Ipsos-Reid/Cook	10/28-31	17
6. Zogby/Reuters	10/26-29	27
7. Harris/Time/CNN	10/23-24	17
8. OpinionDyn/FOX news	10/22-23	36
9. Hart-Teeter/WSJ/NBC news	10/18-21	13
10. PrincetonSRA/Pew	10/17-27	23
11. Harris	10/15-21	<u>19</u>
		311

Table 2 shows the responses to the most recent asking of each organization (listed in the same order as in Tables 1 and 3). The percent of the public who don't answer the question or give no answer, or say they are not sure or, as in (5), have "mixed feelings", are recorded under the catch-all, DK.

Table 2 Responses to most recent asking. Organizations in same order as in Table 1.

Organiz-ations	Percentages			Population Sampled	Wording Variations
	Approve	Disapprove	DK		
1	68	27	5	Adults	
2.	60	30	10	Adults	
3.	61	30	9	Likely Voters	
4.	67	32	1	Likely Voters	
5.	64	34	2	Adults	"mixed feelings"
6.	64	35	1	Likely Voters	
7.	61	33	6	Adults	"In general"
8.	60	30	10	Likely Voters	
9.	63	31	6	Registered Voters	"In general"
10.	59	29	12	Adults	
11.	64	35	1	Adults	*

In all eleven surveys, the populations sampled are as indicated: either all "adults" (over 18), people who say they are "likely to vote", or "registered voters".

There also were slightly different question wording in the most recent asking of all 11 organizations. In surveys (7) and (9) the phrase "In general" was included as the first words of the question. In the Harris poll (11) the public responses allowed were: "excellent", "pretty good", "only fair", or "poor". As frequently done "excellent" and "pretty good" were combined under "approve", while "only fair" and "poor" were combined under "disapprove".

A clue to the importance of probing the DKs was uncovered by further research revealing that organizations, (4), (6) and (11) who have 1% DK in Table 2, generally obtained very low DKs when they repeatedly asked the question earlier. The four organizations with DKs ranging from 9% to 12%, similarly had large DKs when they asked the same question earlier.

A polling organization that wants small DKs asks its field house to "probe the DKs", which requires them to use a number of techniques to increase either "approve" or "disapprove" responses and reduce DKs. Techniques include: (1) waiting patiently for an answer (2) after a long time encouraging a substantive, not a DK answer, by saying a neutral colloquial phrase like, "Well, whad'ya think?" (3) being willing to call back later if respondent feels rushed, (4) reminding respondents that the survey results are important in determining what kind of governance we'll all get in the future.

Those pollsters who need to meet short deadlines, or put their interviewers on hourly quotas, or want their costs as low as possible (the shorter the survey, the less it costs the sponsor) want an interviewer to give the respondent almost no thinking time. After a second or two interviewer impatiently says, "Don't know? That's OK". Most respondents assent, and it's on to the next question. Another reason for encouraging a quick DK response, is ideology. Many organizations sincerely believe that the general public knows little about anything as important as politics. For some or all of these reasons, certain organizations prefer large DKs.

In each of the eleven rows of Table 2, the ratio of "approve" to "disapprove" is close to two to one. Table 3 results are derived from Table 2 values by splitting the percentage points of each DK in the two to one ratio and adding those points to the "approve" and "disapprove" percentages in the same row, rounding off fractional points for best-fit. For example, the third row DK is 9. 9, split 2 to 1, is 6 and 3. 6 is added to "approve" and 3 is added to "disapprove", making them 67 and 33 with DK reduced to zero. If the DK is not divisible by 3 without fractions, such as in row 1, where it is 5, we get five divided 2 to 1 is 3.33 and 1.67, which rounds off to 3 and 2, when added to the "approve" and "disapprove" percentages and give exactly what is shown in Table 3. This procedure, called allocating the DKs, is based on the idea that those who respond to the question have roughly the same preference ratio as those who explicitly choose their responses for either "approve" or "disapprove". Allocating the DKs successfully in an increasing number of cases develops empirical evidence to substantiate the validity of the idea.

Table 3. Responses, most recent asking, "Don't Knows" allocated to 0.

Organizations	Approve	Disapprove
1.	71	29
2	66	34
3.	67	33
4.	67	33
5.	65	35
6.	65	35
7.	65	35
8.	66	34
9.	67	33
10.	67	33
11.	65	35

Look at Table 3. At the top, (1) is anomalous: 4 points (or more) higher for "approve", and 4 points (or more) lower for "disapprove", than any of the other 10 cases. The 10 are each within ±1 point of 66% "approve" and 34% "disapprove". Was there something momentous that happened before (1) was in the field and after (2)-(11) had been completed? Yes there was. The UN Security Council unanimously approved the Iraq resolution wanted by Bush to make it clear that the "whole world was behind the US", a very important forward step for Bush's evolving pre-emptive policy. Bush's approval rating went up significantly after his big UN win. If we had not allocated the DKs, the distinction of the Gallup result, would have been almost unnoticeable in Table 2.

We have shown empirically that the variation in responses in Table 2 that theoretically might be due to four differences among the 11 surveys can be ascribed to a sampling error of only ±1%, not the usual ±3%, and within that small error, the facts that (A) the field dates of the 11 surveys were not exactly the same, but stretched over a short 24-day period. (B) The populations sampled varied and (C) the exact wording varied somewhat – are all immaterial.

Allocating DKs is useful, makes polling results more consistent, and sometimes tells us something important that would be totally lost. I'm for it. There is no standard behavior in the polling industry about whether or how to probe the DKs. Pollsters feel they have enough trouble fending off hecklers and critics who question many of the weaknesses of bad polling, such things as high discontinuance rates. They do not relish trying to explain what they do about "probing the DKs", let alone why it is a problem. A famous, honest pollster, Fred Steeper, who can be credited with the election of George W. Bush and W's father before him, called the problem of probing the DKs "the dirty little secret of polling".

Now, the reader who has completed this chapter is way ahead of political junkies and leading politicians too. Both of these groups with very few exceptions don't know about "the dirty little secret".

. . . .

Summarizing our findings in this chapter: The three easy ways that help spot spin are these:

1. There is spin if the media don't report enough for you to figure the size of the DKs

2. There is spin if the DKs are large, particularly for the kind of question being asked
      There is spin if the "Volunteered" is large, but you can correct for it.

3. There is spin (a) if only one choice is offered, and (b) if only two choices are offered while "neither" and/or "both" are omitted, and (c) if any choice is omitted that common sense tells you should be there, even if it does not score well.

Chapter 6   Fair Response Choices – Equal *Weight* and *Coherence*

In Chapter 2 we saw how complex and unusable the full response could be to a single either-or question of the type "Favor A or B?" A very wise, hypothetical respondent was willing to explain to the interviewer under precisely which conditions s/he would favor each of the four choices: only A, only B, both, and neither. One very clear conclusion, confirmed again on pp. 48-49 and 59, is that if "neither" and "both" are not offered as acceptable answers, the media poll report could be misleading and spinful, i.e., sinful.

In Chapter 5, pp. 49-50, we saw how even more unfair is the *choiceless* choice question, "Favor A? yes or no?", and how you can spot the more subtle spin of the sponsor-favored choice A, beefed up to be stronger and more compelling than alternatives B, C, etc. We explained the method by which poll designers can be almost certain that the choices offered, A, B, C, etc., are fairly presented, with minimal imbalance and minimal bias. All of the different techniques for keeping the various multiple choices offered in a survey question as fair, unbiased, and balanced as possible, provide choices of what is summarized with the phrase *"equal weight"*.

Combinations of Two Statements/Items in a Response Choice

So far we have considered choices A and B that are each a single item or a single statement. However, A and B may be two (or more) different and, at least somewhat, unrelated statements and items. Question Q12 from a Hart-Teeter survey, conducted Feb. 20-24, 1997 for *the Council on Excellence in Government,* is a good example.

For background, Democrat Peter Hart and Republican Bob Teeter are a prominent polling team, whose poll findings often appear in the Wall Street Journal and elsewhere. Bob Teeter was the Republican pollster for the ATI polling team in its early days, until he resigned to become a top advisor to the successful Bush campaign for President in 1988. Here was their question; each choice consists of two different ideas:

Please tell me which one of the following statements about people's attitudes toward the federal government comes closer to your own point of view.
Q12
(A) It's a good thing for America that many people are skeptical about the federal government, and we need to guard against government getting too big and powerful.
Or
(B) It's a bad thing for America that many people are skeptical about the federal government, and we need to appreciate what government does and try to improve it.

Which would you choose, A or B? How about if we rematched the two parts of each substantive choice this way:

(A') It's a good thing for America that many people are skeptical about the federal government, and we need to appreciate what government does and try to improve it.

(B') It's a bad thing for America that many people are skeptical about the federal government, and we need to guard against government getting too big and powerful.

It happens that chapters 12 and 13 of *Locating Consensus for Democracy* get to the bottom of why people mistrust the federal government and why the two political parties and most of Washington do not want to understand the reasons for the public's mistrust. Although the full explanation, examined in the next chapter, is a little more complex, reduced to two alternatives (A") and (B"), these reasons are as follows:

(A") People mistrust the federal government because the government is getting too big and powerful.

(B") People mistrust the federal government because it favors special interests and does not operate in the interests of all the people.

Extensive research showed that the overwhelming majority of the public (>75%) agree with B", a smaller majority agree with A". (implying over 25% agree with both.) Republicans and conservatives lean more to A" than others do.

Did Peter Hart, Bob Teeter or perhaps the poll sponsors think that on this Q12 question good Democrats would agree with A and good Republicans agree with B? ATI results showed that many people, including Republicans and Democrats, would agree as much with A' as with A *and* agree as much with B' as with B, so that conjecture does not stand up. In my opinion if this question were tested with any choices other than A" and B", the findings would be junk.

Cleaning Up Bad Either-Or Questions
You might imagine that either-or questions begging for "both" or "neither" responses are rare. They are not. They are very common. Here is a group of them that appeared in a very high profile poll that was given to a random sample of people both before and after they attended the National Issues Convention in Austin, TX, January 1996. Some of these also appeared in a Washington Post poll shortly thereafter:

Here are some things people think are important. Tell me which one of the two statements comes closer to your feelings on the subject. [Questions are numbered as in the Convention Report]

15. Some people think that America's interests should always come first.
    Others think that people should consider the interests of people in other countries too.

16. Some people think that we should all respect authority.
    Others think that we should all do what we think best, regardless of authority.

17. Some people think that people should be able to do whatever they want with their property.
    Others think that sometimes the community should be able to tell people what they can and can't do with their property.

18. Some people think that no one should be too rich or too poor.
    Others think that everyone should be able to earn and keep as much or as little as he or she can.

19. Some people think that people should make more sacrifices for the future.
    Others think that people should just do the best they can in the present.

20. Some people think that the most important thing in foreign affairs is to get other countries to do what we want.
    Others think that the most important thing in foreign affairs is to act morally.

S3. Some people say that there has been a breakdown in the traditional family.
    Others say that families are just finding new forms.

S4. Some people think that the biggest problem for the American family is economic pressure.
    Others think that it is the breakdown of traditional American values.

S5. Some people think that government has become too involved with the family through social welfare and family planning programs.
    Others think that government has not done enough for the family through child care, family planning and education.

In all these questions if "both", "neither", and "it depends" were read by the interviewers as offered choices along with the question actually asked, "Which do you agree with more?" these additional new choices, collectively, would generally score better than the two, together, actually offered.

Finally, offering a wide range of response choices in a single question (called a *battery* in Chapter 4, p. 38) is a good way to clean up a mess like this.

Combinations of Multiple Statements/Items in One Response Choice
Everything heretofore said to the contrary not withstanding, there can be legitimate
reasons for either-or questions. We illustrate this point with Q8 and Q9 of ATI-21,
Apr. '93. The DKs are 2% and 3%, low enough to indicate that the respondents had
no problem understanding these rather lengthy response choices.

Q8. Now I would like to read you two statements to see which is best.
[After reading statements ask] Please tell me which is closer to the way you think about things]

First, President Bill Clinton supports the idea of maintaining a strong and mobile military,
but he has proposed cutting defense spending by 126 billion dollars over five years, which
amounts to an 8 percent cut averaged over the next five years. The President would use these
savings to reduce the budget deficit and redirect funds to address America's economic needs

38% prefer.

OR

Second, General Colin Powell has proposed cuts in defense spending that are less than
Clinton's. Powell has proposed cuts of 60 billion dollars over five years, a 4 percent average
cut per year. Powell warns against larger cuts because he thinks they would limit America's
ability to respond to crises abroad. **60% prefer.**

Q9. Now I would like to read you two other statements. Please tell me which statement you
agree with more. . . . .

Statement 1. Some people say the US should not rush major cuts in defense spending just
because the Cold War is over. Many foreign leaders are more unpredictable and dangerous
than ever before. The US needs to maintain its current military strength to deal with the
danger of international terrorism, drug trafficking, and weapons of mass destruction falling in
the hands of third world dictators. And major cuts in defense spending will seriously damage
large manufacturers and cost millions of industrial jobs at a time when the economy is in bad
shape.

56% agree

Statement 2. Other people say the end of the Cold War offers a unique opportunity to cut
defense spending. Half of our defense budget went to defend against the Soviet threat, which
no longer exists, and we no longer need the conventional forces that were used to defend
Europe and Japan. We can use these savings to rebuild our economy and convert defense
industries to civilian industries, including worker training and unemployment compensation
for workers laid off by defense contractors.

41% agree

Question Q8 is comprised of fairly exact, short descriptions of views on military policy, one by then President Clinton, widely discredited on military matters as lacking experience, and the second by Colin Powell, then Chairman of the Joint Chiefs and, following the first Gulf war, the most respected US general since Eisenhower. The question is asked as an either-or question, "Which is best?" Yes, there are multiple items in each view, but they all belong to the two leaders with little overlap. It is a fair, accurate and useful question.

The small DK size of 2% (as compared to some large number like 30%) attests to the public's willingness to agree with one side or the other when the sides are clearly defined and politically significant as they are in both questions, Q8 and Q9.

Question Q9 takes out the authority figures from Q8 and states what was a good presentation of their underlying views, the "philosophy" (really "rationale") behind the positions of Clinton and Powell. When the authorities are specifically mentioned in Q8 the preference is for General Powell is a little better than 3 to 2. It is remarkable that when the philosophies of the two leaders are given *without* mentioning their names the ratio of support for Powell's ideas compared to Clinton's ideas was still better than 4 to 3, only a small drop from when the authority figures themselves have been removed from the choice.

If it were true that some different combination of the facts taken from Statements 1 and 2 of Q9 would find a much higher support than the 56% support of Statement 1, we could not learn that from the results of Q8 and Q9. It could be learned systematically by testing the effect of each new idea in the two statements, a tedious but reliable method. I think it unlikely that we would find any support much above 56%, but it is certainly possible, even though unlikely, that there was some not-readily-determined consensus buried away in these findings.

Sometimes multipart choices are useful for understanding public opinion when each such choice is related in the minds of the public to a coherent idea, or a well-known unifying name, or associated by the public with a well-known authority figure. I have called this *"coherence"*. Multipart choices otherwise will uncover little useful data and should be avoided.

Chapter 7. Down Boy? No — Give the People a Break

The poll results that the media show us in newspapers, magazines, TV and radio are supplied by big time commercial pollsters. With their six figure incomes, college plus education, and frequent association with high-level officials, pundits, and moguls, they tend to be elitists. They avoid the public-interest polling techniques we examined in earlier chapters. It seems reasonable to them to confirm their predilections and use question types that put people in their place, unmasking those who may be spouting off without any analysis that backs-up their response choices.

Spin-spotters will enjoy seeing in this chapter the many ways this is done.

On the air pundits know better than to put down "the people". Disparaging the public publicly is the kiss of death for a public personality. So like other elitists frequently in the media spotlight, pollsters often come across on TV as low-key, honest and pleasant, even homey and modest. But pollsters do tend to believe that many people will give you an opinion on almost any subject you throw out to them, that their question answers are knee-jerk responses, not based on thought and knowledge, and that "ordinary" people have *attitudes,* not *reasoned* opinions. So when required to ask questions on issues with any depth and complexity, and especially if the issue is highly controversial because a hotly contested key vote will likely be in the headlines when their latest findings will be released, what do commercial pollsters do to protect themselves?

One simple thing is to offer an additional response choice. At the tail-end of questions, they add:

" -- or don't you know enough to say?"

This is low-key and seems fair, but it can have a big effect on responses. Why and how does this option put spin on polls that undermine the validity of commercial polling?

The name used for this "don't-you-know-enough-to-say" choice is, "Down, boy," a name that suggests what is going on. With complex issues, particularly those unfamiliar to the public, saying in effect, "Down, boy", can change responses enormously. Frequently, 75% of the public will choose it, as we will see in the next section. "Down, boy," narrows rather than broadens the wide range of substantive policy choices with which polling in the public-interest is concerned, but it satisfies the elitist mentality.

An alternative to the "Down, boy" response choice that produces a similar chilling effect comes from asking a preliminary question, called – fair enough -- the "Down, boy" question. An example is this. If A is the policy to be tested and X is the deep complex issue for which A is supposed to be a remedy, the Down Boy question is

(1) "How closely do you follow issue X, very closely, somewhat closely, or hardly at all?"

followed by

(2) "Do you favor or oppose policy A?"

Many of those who do not choose "very closely," typically a majority, will be embarrassed enough to beg off answering the follow-up question (2),

The DKs in the policy question (2) will be much larger than if the "Down, boy" question (1) had been omitted.

Two prominent pollsters, Norbert Schwarz and Howard Schuman, researched this subject a few years ago and in a respected learned journal of survey research a few years ago published an article

"Political Knowledge, Attribution, and Inferred Interest in Politics: the Operation of Buffer Items."

They showed that flunking a knowledge question just before being asked whether respondents know enough about something to have an opinion significantly increases the percentage who opt for "OK. So I'm a dummy."

Still another way for elitist pollsters to say "Down, boy" that works for them in certain questions comes up in the next chapter. These pollsters allow only responses with the phrase, "People like me believe (or other verb) . . .". Carrying an implication or cue that affects responses, the idea is simple but the consequences can be enormous.

Many people are a little embarrassed that they do not follow issues closely or are not presumptuous enough to think they have something important to say about them, unlike the pundits on talk shows who appear to have an enormous knowledge of policies and issues, and also unlike those "ordinary" people who are nervy enough to call into TV/radio shows to ask questions of the guests or make a comment. In survey research respondents are not getting paid. Why should they extend themselves? It is reasonable and modest for them to accept the "Down, boy" cue and opt out or respond "Don't Know", and many do.

Much can be learned from asking the questions without possible cues like "Down, boy" that people interpret as meaning the pollsters *do not want* a substantive answer. We will see how policy questions with and without "Down, boy" work out in Chapter 8, pp. 73-79.

Respondents are Amazing Real People
One of the favorite ways elites have of putting down the public is to present knowledge questions, like "How long is the term of a US Senator?" or "What is the capital of Honduras?" Probably not one in a hundred knows the capital of Honduras. I had to look it up myself – not so easy if you don't know how to spell it – Hunduras, Hondurus. Help, spell check, google. OK, here it is -- Tegucigalpa.

Having spent years wandering through the offices of official Washington, I do know the length of a Senator's term of office, but most people could go all their lives, have a successful career, even vote regularly, and never need to know that particular fact. On knowledge questions that are important to politicians and political scientists or, for that matter, any professional jargon, the public does poorly.

One is tempted to say "abysmally". In fact, that was the very term I used at one presentation and lost half my audience, apparently, a group of true populists. I don't use it anymore, because it is not fair. In order to understand why I say that, let's look at knowledge questions from the point of view of the typical respondent. Before we do that, let's get to know respondents a little in a way that sheds light on how real people feel about being interviewed that came from my own frequent monitoring of survey interviews on a listen-only telephone receiver.

On one occasion a man with a strong, confident voice gave sensible answers to a long survey on policy preferences until the last few questions when he was asked the year of his birth. He had not noticed, or perhaps ignored, the interviewers opening qualifying spiel that asked for "the youngest household member *over 18.*" It turned out he was only 15. The interview had to be discarded.

In another survey about global issues, one of the respondents was very negative about the United Nations. Rooted in the oral social contract where the respondent agrees at the beginning to complete the interview, the process of the interview itself paid off. Both respondent and interviewer continued slogging away with the Q&A. My silent reaction was, "Uh, oh. We've got a real UN hater here." I knew that if I had found myself talking in person with him, I would have expected little but a continuing negative reaction. I would have already changed the subject or walked away. Further along in the interview came a few questions on the UN's role in the protection of women. Surprise. On this one issue, out-of-the-blue the respondent was remarkably *pro*-UN. What a story there must have been behind that. But a more important conclusion is how only the polling interview process and a well-designed survey together could have uncovered that obscure and seemingly odd fact.

Another story serves two purposes. A woman answers the phone, and I hear the interviewer in her most professional tone read from the CATI screen:

> "Hello, my name is (*caller name*). I'm calling for ATI, a non-profit foundation. I would like to ask you a few questions concerning the problems facing our nation, state and local communities. We are *NOT* selling anything, and I will *NOT* ask you for a donation. Since this is a scientific survey, we need a balance of men and women. May I speak to the youngest man, 18 years or older, *who is at home right now?*"

Then I hear the voice of the woman at home turned away from the phone, quite loud and dripping with sarcasm: "Honey, your sweetie pie is on the line."

One more – a woman answering a similar opening by an interviewer with

> "Well, it's about time. You people've called everybody. Now, it's
> my turn. What d'ya want to know?"

The two purposes? Oh, (1) as we design questions meeting a host of criteria, it reminds us that the people being interviewed, the respondents, are real people with enormously diverse personalities, knowledge, and interests, and (2) you've just read a typical interviewer's introduction, which is an offer to get a respondent to commit to being interviewed. It implies that the survey sponsor seriously wants to know what the people think, and there will be no tricks, no embarrassments, and no questions that a typical respondent could not reasonably be expected to be able to answer. When the respondent agrees to the interview there is created a verbal contract to the effect that the respondent will answer to the best of his/her ability and the interviewer will live up to his/her introductory offer.

It is true that the two parties have little to lose if the contract is broken. Certainly the respondent can hang up and forget about it. Since the sponsor then will lose a few bucks and gets no interview, the respondent who accepts the offer has reason to be optimistic. So the questions start. Let's assume for a while that the questions are easy and reasonable from the respondent's point of view. Then the first knowledge question breaks the contract. Why? Let the respondent explain.

Real People Reactions to Knowledge Questions.
Here is the respondent's case, bluntly stated.

> "Well, sir/ma'am, why are you asking me a question whose answer you
> could better find out from a research library? I don't have to take any
> damn test from you. I could ask you some questions you couldn't answer,
> too. This is like the pop quizzes some smart-ass teachers loved to pull off.
> Or those job aptitude tests we sometimes got that had little to do with what
> the job actually required. I bet you didn't like them anymore than anybody
> else. I only remember what is important to me in my life and that is
> plenty. Yeah, I might be able to answer some of these questions, but why
> should I? And by the way, this is not personal. I know you are just a hard
> working guy/gal like the rest of us. But tell this to your sponsor."

I am not implying that any of those thoughts actually are going through the mind of a respondent at that moment, but people have a sixth sense about when others have baited and switched. When they realize that is just what has happened, the attitudes of many change. Some may start giving garbage answers. The attention of others may slack off. It isn't fun anymore. The public is diverse, of course, and for others a knowledge question may be welcome.

Some may actually *enjoy* taking the knowledge test – the ex-teacher's pets who have not had a chance to show off how good they are at tests since their last school year, which was, for the average respondent, twelve years earlier. But even they are at a disadvantage, which the elites ignore when poll results uncover the "ignorance of the public." Interrupted from home activities with their minds on other things, respondents living in the "attention-deficit society" as we all are, cannot deal well with the pop quiz on political knowledge. Experts, when their minds are on other things, may not do much better.

It is a cheap shot for anyone to use knowledge question findings to put down the public as foolish or dumb. But politicians sometimes find it useful to try to deflect any heat arising from poll results that could put them at odds with the public by implying that poll results are generally misleading (not true) and that polls make people look foolish. The news media can use that same rationale to justify dismissing results the editors and gatekeepers dislike or find dubious.

Reactions to Breaking-News Stories
A closely related cheap shot occurs when reporters and pundits do not know how to evaluate a breaking news story where few facts are yet available. So in a few hours they do a quickie poll of the public with some question like, "Did the navy do the right thing shooting down the Iranian airliner yesterday?" This is amusing. The media hotshots do not know how to play the story themselves, so they decide to throw the ball to the public. This kind of question should be ruled off-limits in public-interest polling as a knowledge question *or* as an *evaluation* question. The public has no more aptitude for evaluating fleeting incidents than the news media.

A *hard* knowledge question, say on a quiz show, is one that few people know the answer to, like "What is the capital of Honduras?" That produces over 90% "Don't knows". A hard question in public-interest polling is one where the respondent has difficulty choosing the response from those offered, sometimes because the question is confusing or unintelligible, sometimes because it takes a little thought to choose the answer, and sometimes because the choices offered are inadequate. Fortunately, in ATI surveys, all of these are relatively rare. If "What is the capital of Honduras?" were asked in an ATI survey where there are no right or wrong answers, it would be a relatively *easy* question for most people to answer by the ATI definition. For most people the right answer is clearly "Don't Know". Knowledge questions should be asked rarely in surveys.

If a survey asks a lot of knowledge questions, it is a sure sign that the results will be made public in order to put down the public, and minimize the impact of public opinion on what the leaders are planning to do with or without public support. Does this really happen? A prominent example arose in January of 1996 when Washington Post survey results appeared for five consecutive days in long articles, leading with front-page headlines. Earlier surveys including several by ATI had shown that mistrust of official Washington was at an all time high for a simple reason, the government was not doing what most people, with good reason, wanted. Clearly the Post editors believed that the public's mistrust was unfair to all the hardworking bureaucrats, officials, journalists, lobbyists, lawyers and politicians who depended on the Post as *their* paper.

The Post articles presented the results to make the case that the mistrust was really no worse than it had always been, that the public was more mistrustful of all institutions, that people mistrusted each other more, and of course, that the public did not know enough to have valid opinions on the difficult issues that the government was dealing with. Old knowledge questions that had been asked over the years were asked again, and without showing that the public's knowledge was *less* than it used to be (it wasn't), the Washington Post wrapped it up with data that implied "You (the public) don't trust us. Well, we don't trust you much either." Of course such words, putting down the public explicitly, never appeared in the paper in print.

The Washington Post effort to defuse the antagonism between the inner circle of the Beltway and the rest of the country crashed in vain before the end of the year when the Clinton era scandals broke over the sale to big money contributors of overnights in the Lincoln bedroom, breakfasts and coffees in the White House and equivalent shenanigans in the House and Senate. The justified perception of corruption is rampant everywhere now, but not then. The Republicans blasted what President Clinton did in 1995, but now by 2001, the same behavior is, when conducted quietly, "accepted", if not "acceptable."

When asked by a reporter, what was the difference between the fund raising that Bush was engaging in with fat-cats in the White House, including many specifics like "overnights in the Lincoln bedroom", Ari Fleischer, spokesperson for Bush in 2001, dismissed the reporter with a simple, "We haven't had overnight's in the Lincoln bedroom." Fleischer did not deny all the other similarities of selling White House access between the two parties, who often act like two football teams with the same owner.

Chapter 8. Let the scales be right. Let them drop from your eyes.

Making Good Use of Numerical and Commonly-Used Word Scales
If a pollster asks, "On a scale of one to ten, how do you feel about Bill Gates?", he gets some lively answers, like:
"He is great! Give him a <u>ten</u>."
"I hate what the Internet has done to our business. He's a <u>one</u> in my book."
"I'm not involved in any of that stuff. I'm neutral. Give him a <u>five.</u>"

A scale, like "one-to-ten" brings out the great variety of people's reactions better than the conventional "either-or" way to ask that question:
"Do you like or dislike Bill Gates, Chairman of Microsoft?"

Unfortunately, though it rolls off the tongue, the one-to-ten scale is not one of the better scales, as we will see.

Can scales and other different kinds of response choices that pollsters use put a spin on the poll? You bet they can. Let's first see how scales came to be used, what's good and bad about scales, and how they produce spin.

When people in survey interviews are asked a typical either-or question, as we have seen, the lack of choices often produces large DKs. But there is something else going on. In a question with only two choices, "agree" or "disagree", people sometimes do not feel strongly about the underlying issue. How they do feel can best be described this way. Flatly saying either "agree" or "disagree," they feel, would overstate their position. This moves them to opt for their only remaining choice, DK. Pollsters have moved to accommodate such respondents by expanding their substantive choices from two to four along a "strongly/somewhat" dimension, like this: (1) strongly agree, (2) somewhat agree, (3) somewhat disagree, and (4) strongly agree. DK then becomes choice (5). This takes care of the needs of those who only *somewhat* agree/disagree, and that generally includes virtually all respondents. Very few feel strongly on every agree/disagree question in a survey with many such questions.

This five point scale also adds a whole new usefulness to the public's response to a poll question. It allows pollsters to measure what in polling lingo is called **"salience"**. If two policies that are alternative ways to deal with an issue both have large support, say, 80%, pollsters sometimes find amazingly big differences in the strength of that support, as much as 60% **strongly** and 20% **somewhat** flipping to 20% **strongly** and 60% **somewhat**. A policy with 60% strong support is said to be more **salient** than one with 20% strong support.

When respondents really feel neutral about an issue, they would prefer to have a "neutral" choice explicitly allowed. Why is this important? There are some poll questions where "neutral," when offered, captures the plurality, even a majority. An example from ATI#18 is:

Q24. "Should social security taxes be cut, increased or kept the same?"
Response: Cut 14%; Increased 20%; Kept the same 64%.

Those responding "cut" or "increased," were asked, "By how many billions of dollars?"

The four-point scale (not counting DK), when augmented with a "neutral" option is improved and becomes a five-point scale (one to five) with the neutral point at three, clearly in the middle. Some respondents respond to a policy or issue question, by thinking, "On this one I'm in the middle," and they'll choose "three" because of that.

Scales with an even number of points, like ten, do not have a middle value to represent neutral, while odd scales do. As a courtesy for the respondents, to anchor the middle value as the neutral point, odd scales (like five or seven point scales) are desirable.

A further step in this direction is illustrated by the following question introduction: The interviewer reads off the CATI screen these words, "On a scale of one to seven, where one means "very opposed", four is "neutral" and seven is "very favorable", how would you rate ...*whatever* ?" This seven point scale was defined or "anchored" only at three points, the two extremes and the neutral point. People have no trouble understanding and using seven point scales anchored at only three points, and even those anchored at only the two extreme points, as the following example illustrates:

With the next larger odd-point scales (nine or eleven), it becomes unclear that the public can be making useful distinctions. Is there any real difference on a nine or eleven point scale between the attitude of the person who chooses 6 from the one who chooses 7? Coming from many questions asked both ways, the answer is "very little". Tests have also shown that responses are hardly changed when a question is asked first with a seven point numerical scale and then in another survey with the same question but only a two point, favor or oppose, response scale. It turns out that the percent of persons choosing "5, 6, or 7", in the first case will be close to the percent choosing "favor" in the second. In practice, the two different scales do not lead to much different results. Polls with large scales create some data that verges on the useless or misleading. The one-to-ten scale has this problem and that's a second reason that it is not so good.

In any "for or against" question, including "yes/no", "favor/oppose", "agree/disagree", "approve/disapprove", "do/do not support", it is better to use a seven point scale running from minus three to plus three, where zero is neutral, minus three is very opposed and plus three is very favorable (thereby anchored at three points). Zero is a natural anchor for neutrals. Negative numbers are appropriate for people who are negative on the question and positive numbers are appropriate for people who are positive on the question. Do negative numbers bother people? Not really. Today people have no more trouble with negative numbers than they have with dealing with weather forecasts of 14 below zero in Minneapolis, at least if they are in Florida watching it all on TV. Beyond that, there is a definite plus for the zero centered, seven point scale, where no number greater than three need ever be mentioned. Dealing with a scale that is "as simple as 1, 2, 3" is better than one that is a little harder for the innumerate. Who has ever heard someone say, "It's as simple as 1, 2, 3, 4, 5, 6, 7"? Case closed.

So altogether the old one-to-ten scale is not up to snuff on three counts. It's even, not odd; it's a bit large; and it is all positive. But that scale and most other numerical scales have one thing going for them. They don't add spin. Spin is to be found in *non-numerical* scales, and they are important when the political stakes are high.

Manipulation of Non-Numerical Scales for Political Purposes
We are talking about spinning political poll questions planned for public release, purporting to explain what the public itself wants. Often these are *"high profile"* polls that play a key role in a public relations campaign designed to have a major impact on the political agenda of the country. Such campaigns can succeed in setting or changing the agenda. They can make front page headlines.

A high profile poll can be many thousands of times more significant than most of the hundred or so polls that policy organizations release every year and typically are never seen or heard about by more than a million people. This sounds like a large number, but is less than one half of 1% of the people of the United States. The typical poll disappears from public view within a few days, forgotten by all but a relatively minuscule few people who are poll watchers.

A high profile poll alone cannot affect a significant percentage of Americans. It *can* serve as the keystone in the arch of the campaign that does have such an impact. If its sponsors have enough political clout, funding, and mainstream news media access, the campaign can be that kind of a huge success. The high profile poll's legitimacy is used to assure the elites that the American people are behind whatever it is that the sponsors are aiming for. The critical role of high profile polling is that it becomes a key element of the campaign that makes history.

The high profile poll sponsor, or some of its sponsors, or some of the key individuals representing a sponsor, are generally aiming higher than just getting some specific legislation enacted. They aim to keep the US favorable to their own interests or visions, essentially to shape the future of the country, the nature of our government and our society. They may be looking to control the definition of what it means to be an American, a definition that may be very different in the future from what it has been in the past. Some seek a definition of an America that somehow does not change even if change seems to many to be required ultimately for the prosperity of the US, even someday our very survival.

The sponsors are the special interests who may truly believe that their cause is America's cause, that their view must prevail. The campaign may be remarkably successful, even though the high profile polling it depends on may be misleading. The polling may produce some findings that are completely erroneous, or are deliberately and stealthily steered during the design, analysis and/or promotion phases into engineering consent for whatever the controlling individuals are seeking.

Let us look at some examples of high profile polls that falsified the voice of the people by the misleading use of scales. One poll, mentioned in Chapter 6, p. 58, was given twice to a random sample of people both before and after they attended the National Issues Convention (NIC) in Austin, TX, January 1996. The concept that was being tested by the NIC, was that after a weekend of deliberation on political issues, "ordinary" people would make better choices.

Unbalanced Scales
These NIC survey question choices, I do believe were not chosen as part of a plan to change America, but rather were inadvertent and incompetent.

These results show how unbalanced response scales will pull answers toward the side with more options. Question S11 of the NIC survey had a five point scale, three on one side – "extremely," "very," and "somewhat willing" – and two on the other – "not very" and "never willing." The neutral point was not in the middle.

Here were the responses to the same poll asked before and after the Convention:

S11. In the future, how willing should the United States be to send troops to solve problems in other countries?

	Before	After
	Convention	
Extremely willing	2%	6%
Very willing	8%	12%
Somewhat willing	53%	55%
Not very willing	24%	22%
Never willing	6%	2%

A fair fraction of respondents do not pay much attention to the interviewer's instructions, which define the scale. The words, "extremely, "very", "somewhat", "not very", and "never" flow by them quickly. Few realize as the list of choices is read that the middle choice is not neutral. As has been mentioned, many respond as if their thought process was something like, "On this one I'm in the middle," and "On that one I'm at the top." If this kind of thinking were the dominant factor, then "somewhat willing," the middle category, should be counted as neutral; if not, "somewhat willing," by the meaning of the words themselves, should be counted among the willing. In the former case, the conclusion is only "10% are willing". In the latter case the conclusion is "63% are willing". A big difference. Because of the five-point scale without the middle choice clearly being "neutral," all we can know for sure from this question is that the public is somewhere between 10% and 63% willing *before* and between 18% and 73% *after* the Convention– an enormous range. The finding is not informative. It's really a joke.

What is informative is a small increase in willingness overall from "before" to "after" deliberation. What constituted those deliberations and what was their effect? The answer is wrapped up in the next section.

People Like Me
Questions that might otherwise be all right have potential problems for deliberative survey usage. Three questions included in the National Issues Convention (NIC) were:

1a. People *like me* don't have any say about what the government does.

	Before	After
	Deliberation	
Agree strongly	18%	6%
Agree somewhat	26%	25%
Disagree somewhat	31%	32%
Disagree strongly	25%	36%

1b. Public officials care a lot about what people *like me* think.

	Before	After
	Deliberation	
Agree strongly	7%	11%
Agree somewhat	34%	49%
Disagree somewhat	37%	30%
Disagree strongly	19%	9%

1c. Sometimes politics and government seem so complicated that a person *like me* can't really understand what's going on.

	Before	After
	Deliberation	
Agree strongly	18%	17%
Agree somewhat	37%	42%
Disagree somewhat	23%	22%
Disagree strongly	20%	18%

Questions 1a and 1b were cited as evidence that the NIC "empowered" participants, that after deliberating for a weekend, people believed that leaders paid more attention to them because they were smartened up by the wisdom received from the deliberation. At over $8,000 per head as the cost of the Convention to the organizers, this model of empowerment holds little promise for citizens at large. But what was really going on was yet another way of producing the "Down, boy" effect, first discussed in the last chapter.

"What did "people like me" mean to a person who had to answer a survey question before the Convention not just for him/herself but on behalf of "people like me"? The elitists who organized and funded the Convention thought of "average" people or "ordinary" people without realizing the great range of diversity of respondents who were to participate in the Convention, a group as diverse as America itself, if the sampling was properly performed.

At the Convention, participants met with and were addressed by leading politicians of both political parties and by well-known news media reporters and editors. The thinking of participants had to shift in the "after" survey toward "a person like me" as being one whose opinion is valued by the high and mighty who are speaking to us here, lecturing us, and listening to our responses, as well as arranging for

74 −Ch. 8−

televised proceedings, broadcast airtime on major channels, and paying for the weekend excursion of a thousand people to Austin from all around the country. No one can say definitively whether the before and after response shifts were due to the various activities at the convention that were called "deliberation" or for the shift in thinking about who are people "like me". More recent research strengthens the case for the latter.

The Contract with America

In the fall of 1994 shortly before the election, the Republicans in Congress led by Newt Gingrich announced to the media a proposed deal. If the American people elected a Republican Congress, the Republicans would make every effort to enact into law ten policy proposals favored by the public, according to a poll that they had taken. In the month before the election the Republicans waged a campaign to get media coverage of what they called the "Contract with America". The campaign was not very compelling. It is not surprising that the media treated it like a poor publicity stunt and they ignored it.

The next month, when the Republicans swept into power, the press tried to make up for their earlier inattention by calling the victory a landslide, christened it the Republican Revolution, referred to the Contract in words that suggested a sacred text, followed the ten contract items like ten horse races for the next year or so and gave the Republicans tens of millions of dollars of free publicity. Actually, in the 1994 election only slightly more than 2% of voters shifted from Democrat to Republican compared to 1992. The Republicans did not get a majority of registered voters in 1994. The turnout, in fact, was on the low side.

The Republicans never released a survey showing that the public supported all the items of the Contract. They claimed that they hired Frank Luntz, the erstwhile Perot pollster, to do so. Luntz, about a year later, when pressed, explained to an enterprising Knight-Ridder reporter, Frank Greve, that he had only tested item wording for the purpose of advertising slogans and found 60% support for them as catchy slogans, not for favoring legislation. The Republican leaders no doubt felt, on the basis of the rhetoric they used with each other, that the public surely must favor these ideas.

The October 3, '94, *USA Today* edition listed the Contract items as:

1. A balanced budget amendment.
2. "Anti-crime" measures, including tougher sentencing and death penalty rules, and more prisons.
3. Cuts in welfare spending and a ban on welfare for minor-age mothers.
4. "Family reinforcement" measures, including a tax credit for elderly care.
5. A $500-per-child tax credit.
6. Increased defense spending to restore "essential parts of our national security."
7. Repeal of 1993 increase in taxation of upper-income individuals' Social Security benefits.
8. A cut in the tax on capital gains.
9. Limits on punitive damages from civil suits; reform of product liability laws.
10. Congressional term limits.

The Significance of the Contract

The campaign helped to create the Republican Revolution, which passed dozens of bills that did change the course of the nation. The fact that some of the poll items were not supported by the public when tested by other pollsters was ignored by the media and by the Democrats and by Ross Perot's Reform party.

The guilty parties were not only the Republican party, which created the outrageous fallacy of the Contract, the claim of large public support for every item. Also at fault were the Democratic party and Perot's Reform party, which having utilized no better polling than the Republicans on what the American people wanted, left the fallacy unchallenged during and after the campaign. Finally, the mainstream news media can be blamed as well. They neglected the counter-findings of other pollsters, including the balanced teams of pollsters working for ATI in Surveys #22, #24, and #28.

So can you spot the spin on the Republicans' poll? You might think it tough to do, since it was only a virtual poll. That fact in itself is big-time spinning or lying *by omission*, mentioned in Chapters 1, 3 and 5 as the favorite method of spinning or burying undesired news stories by the media and by political leaders. But the ten Contract items were even more virtual than that. After October 3rd, and throughout the following year, the Republicans substituted different items for the ten above. The only consistency in this sea of change was that there were always *ten* items. This public relations technique helped to implant the idea in the minds of the media that the Contract had the timeless saliency of the Ten Commandments.

But this book is about spin. Look at those initial ten items. Plenty of spin there. No size of "Don't Know"s. No scales. No specific question wording. Which of the ten might be supported by a majority of Americans with some fair and balanced wording? From the results of ATI and many other pollsters, the list would go something like this:

Supported: 4, 5, 10
Support definitely depends on wording: 1, 2, 3, 9,
Not supported: 6, 7, 8.

A pretty poor score for a set of policies that the media -- without even knowing the question wording -- reported were favorites with the public.

The '92 and '96 Perot Campaigns

In the '92 presidential campaign, Perot assumed a populist stance, in agreement with what public interest polling teaches, that the people are justified in believing that elected officials of both parties are beholden to special interests, out of touch with the people, and interested primarily in their own careers, incomes, and elections. Perot had for many years before 1992 championed *electronic town meetings* and promised that the cornerstone of his administration would be listening to the voice of the people.

What Perot failed to mention was that, like the leaders of the two major parties and almost all politicians, he did not believe it necessary to do good survey research in order to know what people wanted. Being very smart and politically in tune with crowds, he believed that he already knew what the people wanted, although he was careful to never say that directly. As the great salesman he was, both at Electronic Data Systems and later, he knew how to sway prospects and other audiences by language, tone, demeanor, etc., and how to recover if he did not get it quite right, which occasionally happens to even great salesmen.

In March of '93, Perot conducted his first and only electronic town meeting – widely advertised and promoted – in a half hour purchased from ABC TV, which he turned into an infomercial, whose centerpiece was his Reform party poll on what people wanted for governance.

Many of Perot's proposed policies were presented as all favorable and thus scored well with the public. They had the spin of the *choiceless choice*. You remember Mrs., Thatcher's "There Is No Alternative" in Chapter 5, p. 48. No more than any of the major party leaders, did Perot really want to know and conform to the people's more sensible desires. Perot was no populist.

Here is an example to illustrate this point. Ross Perot's campaign finance reform question, Q1, found 80% support, which Perot took as a mandate for his campaign:

Q1 (Perot). Should laws be passed to eliminate all possibilities of special interests giving huge sums of money to candidates?

The bias of Q1, the lack of any negative statement about Perot's proposal in the question or in a preamble, was rightly challenged by a highly regarded professional pollster, Warren Mitofsky, Executive Director of the organization supplying exit polling for four TV networks in campaign '92. Mitofsky submitted an op-ed letter in the *New York Times* which appeared with a five-column banner proclaiming, "Mr. Perot, You're No Pollster." Because Perot's was a high profile poll with a lot of political significance, the Times published Mitofsky's letter that compared Perot's result to a Time/CNN poll that found only 40% favorable. Mitofsky considered this Time/CNN poll comparable and because it contained a counter-argument, "more balanced,"

Q2 (Time/CNN). Should laws be passed to prohibit interest groups from contributing to campaigns or do groups have a right to contribute to the candidates they support?

However, note that Time/CNN had watered down Perot's proposal by eliminating two features that gave it strength in the minds of the public: (1) "...eliminate all possibilities..." (i.e., NO loopholes) and (2) "huge sums" (NOT small sums). The public is well aware that reform laws are passed with loopholes, which make them ineffective, and is well aware that the problem in campaign financing is not small contributions but "huge sums." Perot was not talking about small sums. Some of the drop in support for Perot's proposal came from weakening it and some from the counter-argument, which loomed stronger precisely because Perot's proposal was weakened. This illustrates a concept, first mentioned in Chapter 5, pp. 49-50: Setting up a comparison of a weakly supported policy B to a policy A, which is a weakened version of a highly favored policy A', increases support for B to the point where B is favored over A, while A' is favored over B. Stated this way, it is clear that trying to get people to think that A and A' are the same, when they are not, is wicked.

But Perot's favored proposals did not score always so well. ATI tested a question with Perot's wording:

Perot. 59% favored "Pass a balanced budget amendment to the Constitution with emergency funds limited exclusively to national defense."

ATI had also obtained the following result with slightly different wording:
ATI. 72% favored, "Pass a balanced budget amendment to the Constitution with emergency funds exclusively to major national disasters."

Worded slightly differently by enlarging "national defense" to "major national disasters" and scoring 72-59=13 points higher, this ATI poll question showed that Perot's pat wording was a bit oversimplified. Perot's failure to note the strength of "major national disasters" and probably of several other exceptions illustrates again that Perot was not interested in finding policies most wanted by the people.

To give Perot his due, a question using Perot's wording scored the highest when tested against over fifty different proposals for government reform in several ATI surveys. It was favored by 80% as follows:

80% favored, "Reduce the salary and benefits of Members of Congress to let them know that we really want spending cuts and that cuts should start at the top with themselves."

We will see in later chapters still other spin techniques used in high profile polls to make monkeys of the media. Stay tuned.

Chapter 9 Asking the Right Questions and Asking the Questions Right

Is the Federal Government Too Big or Too Small?

An aspect of government that leaders most dispute is its proper size. (In modern times, leaders do not debate. They dispute.) The Republicans, when out of power, squealed at how bloated government had become. They became the party of small government and still talk about making government smaller even as Republican leaders build up the federal government larger than ever. The cowed Democrats, whether in or out of power, are quick to apologize when their proposals seem to increase the power or size of government.

And yet, those who are familiar with successful government programs like Treasury Direct or Social Security Benefit Distribution generally would like such programs to have adequate staff and resources to keep up their good service at low cost.

Anyone believing that government is intrinsically unable to do a good job of course would want to shrink it down indefinitely. Anyone in irresolvable doubt about a political program, might opt to cut it and at least save the taxpayers expense. But that doesn't fly for the public. The people think entirely differently.

The Public Goes for the Right Size

The public has a simple and commendable approach to sizing any government activity. If a poll asks whether an ongoing government activity whose purpose is approved by most people should be (1) cut, (2) enlarged, or (3) the right size to do the job, the public goes overwhelmingly for "the right size". In their efforts to distinguish themselves from the other party in closely fought campaigns, both the Democrats and the Republicans since about 1980 have become more ideologically polarized and less willing to consider new ideas. The public is much less polarized.

Poll questions have to be the right size to do their job too. To put a complicated proposal into language that the average person can understand is a challenge that wordsmiths love. From the first draft of a new public-interest polling questionnaire to the final draft, polls typically go through 20 revisions, as the various people involved, the pollsters, the issue experts, the analysts, the sponsor(s), want to pass on question wording.

The Art of Question Design

The question cannot be too wordy. Every word in it can remain only if it serves a required function. Ideas and phrases in the question should be in a logical, understandable order. Long sentences may have to be broken up. With rare exceptions, technical and academic words must be scrapped when a more common word will do. Common short words, particularly verb/nouns like "run", when used with specific prepositions, adverbs, etc., have multiple meanings that are well understood and easily distinguished in context by ordinary people. Such short words can be very useful. People who have the common touch, who can cleverly mimic the speech of many different random persons are helpful in finding good language to express the required ideas. Notice how much these recommendations parallel the question design features that, if all present, lead to small DKs. (See first page 44, Chapter 5.)

Commonly understood metaphors and colloquialisms are OK if they really fill the need. Some think that such phrases are good because everybody is familiar with them. Usually ordinary English can be formulated to achieve something equivalent to a colloquialism but clearer and more accurate. Experts, as they get comfortable in their professional language, have trouble with the ordinary language of the public, rich though it may be, and tend to use even common words with meaning somewhat different from what the public expects.

An example of expert bias that also illustrates the value of *equal weight* choices came in a nuclear weapons survey that asked:

(1) Should the goal of the US be to

(a) eliminate all nuclear weapons,
(b) greatly reduce the number of weapons,
(c) reduce the number by a little,
(d) maintain current levels, or
(e) build new, more advanced nuclear weapons?"

The question appears biased. First because the "no change" option is not the middle choice. But beyond that, choice (e), to balance its *weight* with the *weight* of (a), either (e) should be replaced with something like (e') or (a) be replaced with something closer to, say (a') :

    (e') increase the number of nuclear weapons
    (a') eliminate unnecessary and/or unsafe nuclear weapons.

Another question asked in this survey was,

(2) "Do you think the US should spend more or less money to maintain and *update* its nuclear weapons, or do you think the US is spending about the right amount?"

The desirable features of updated nuclear weapons are described by the Pentagon. They include such things as increased bunker penetration, less weight and greater accuracy, which translate to a capability of killing more people. The "more" response for question (2) was chosen by 23%. If more informative language had been used rather than the bland and positive word *update*, support for "more" would have been reduced. Why is this? In the nuclear expert community a word like *update* is well-understood to mean what the Pentagon means by it, but not so with the public when under the constraints of the poll interview, people have to reply off the top of their head. People think of buying *updated* items this way: if item is broken, rusty, etc., or a new one more reliable, easier to use, safer, or better design, then go for it. In a quick reply people have little chance to think about the deathly aspects of an activity that few have ever thought about, namely *buying* nuclear weapons. If the deadly effects of nuclear weapons were included in the description, the 23% support for spending "more" on nuclear weapons would drop sharply.

Where do the people want to go with nuclear weapons? Chapter 4, page 43, shows that in Dec. '87, Americans opted for total elimination by 56% to 41%. By June '91 the margin had increased further reaching 60% to 38%.

Good Practices in Reading Questions by Interviewers

Words which have multiple meanings or even sound too close to such words, and can be confusing in the context of the question, must be ruled out, since some people may mis-interpret them. Interviewers need to know what words are key to the purpose of the question and have to be clearly heard by all respondents to avoid erroneous responses. Putting such words in CAPS in the interviewer's text is good practice. Words which may be

82

hard to pronounce, like unusual names, must be clarified for the interviewer with a "sounds like" or re-spelled lettering.

Interviewers must be well trained and have an opportunity to rehearse the more difficult new questions. The goal is, "All questions, including preambles and transition statements be understood when read to any respondent (in all their infinite varieties!) by an average interviewer."

Finally it is best to run the questionnaire through a pre-test with 20 or so interviews. Random respondents may find question wording difficulties that emerge and need correcting before the full survey interview schedule begins.

A rule of good survey design is that the interviewer cannot speak too long without allowing the respondent to speak. As an interviewer is speaking, people's thoughts often drop out and become less recallable if opportunities for them to speak are delayed even a few seconds. The statements in a very long question can be broken up into two or more smaller statements by means of a short question, provided of course that the response statistics to the short question appear in the survey report. One way to do this is having the interviewer jump in with:

"Do you understand what I've said?" or " Are you with me?"

The answer is recorded and if it is "no", the interviewer follows up with,

"Let me repeat." or "Let me repeat that. Stop me if I say something not clear to you."

All of this gives the correct impression that the survey sponsor really wants to hear correctly what the respondent's answers are. Taking a poll seriously in this manner, makes the respondent take it more seriously too and keeps him/her responding thoughtfully longer and more accurately than s/he otherwise might do.

Often a policy proposal question is long because the policy has a number of features or items. This presents another opportunity to shorten proposal questions with break points after each item. For example, if you were surveying people on whether they approve of embodying the Ten Commandments into a Constitutional amendment, it is best to ask each separately. One question becomes ten, and the findings are much more useful than a single up-or-down vote on approval of all ten. Maybe a President who is faith-based oriented could get a bill through Congress some day with nine out of the Ten Commandments passed. Pragmatic advisors would tell the President to take it and go for the tenth at a later time.

Long and Short Questions Confirming Findings

The following are a set of questions, some very, very long, that had to be as long as they were in order to make them intelligible to the respondents. How can we tell that they are not too long? As we have seen often before, the DKs are a key clue, and here they are small -- between 2 and 5 percent. The only question with a large DK, 14%, is **B6**, length, surprise, merely 14 words with a 29 word preamble. The longest question is the 143 word **A3**, with a 150 word preamble and a DK of only 4%.

These questions were asked in a survey (ATI-25, '94, some also earlier) on means for funding the UN when members do not pay their dues. The first three **A1-A3** were asked of a random A sample of 519 respondents. The next three **B4-B6** were asked of a different **B** sample of 517. The next question **E7** was asked of both samples, **A** plus **B** totaling 1036 respondents. A good exercise for a wordsmith as s/he looks at these questions is this. Think about whether and how these long questions might be shortened without watering down their meaning. After looking at these questions, we will examine other clues as evidence that they are not too long. Each question set starts with a pre-amble:

Pre-amble for A1-A3. Collecting dues from sovereign nations is tricky and may never work very well. There are ways that the UN could become less dependent on dues. Before we look at these we should realize that many of the big issues of today were not thought about when the UN was founded 50 years ago, for example: environmental pollution, depletion of natural resources, over-population, over-crowded cities, mass migration, drug trafficking, global finance, global manufacturing, and global marketing. Individual nations alone cannot regulate these activities that cross national borders. Increasingly issues are thrown into the lap of the UN which it was never designed to handle. The UN can debate these forever, but it will not be able to do all that the world wants done unless the UN can raise more money. Let's look now at different ways the UN could be funded without depending so much on dues from sovereign nations.

A1. Do you favor or oppose a 1 percent tax by the UN on international air travel which by itself would produce half of all the revenue the UN needs and a savings for all members, which for the US would be about a billion dollars a year. The tax itself would add about a billion dollars to America's international travel and air freight bills. Do you favor or oppose that?

		combined
Strongly favor	32	
Somewhat favor	30	**62**
Somewhat oppose	11	
Strongly oppose	25	**36**
DK	2	

A2. Do you favor or oppose a 1 percent tax on international arms sales and transfers which by itself would produce 10 percent of all the revenue the UN needs and a savings for all members, which for the US would amount to about two hundred million dollars per year. Because the U.S. is the world's largest international arms supplier, this tax would require U.S. arms dealers and their foreign customers, to come up with a considerable sum, estimated at $400 million a year to pay this tax. Do you favor or oppose that?
[IF FAVOR OR OPPOSE] Is that strongly or somewhat (favor/oppose)?

		combined
Strongly favor	45	
Somewhat favor	22	**67**
Somewhat oppose	9	
Strongly oppose	21	**30**
DK	3	

A3. Do you favor or oppose a world-wide tax, proposed by Nobel economics prize winner James Tobin, on international financial speculation in currencies, of ONE-HALF OF ONE PERCENT of the value of trades, which would produce enough revenue to eliminate the dues and assessments of all member states and fund ALL of the UN's needs. This tax would produce in fact a trillion dollars a year which could pay for programs that in a few years would clean up all the world's polluted drinking water supplies, reverse the destruction of all the world's forests, and give a basic education to all the world's children. Some of this tax would fall on international corporations, but, by far, the largest part would fall on financial companies and banks, which do over a trillion dollars worth of such trades EVERY DAY. Do you favor or oppose that? [IF FAVOR OR OPPOSE] Is that strongly or somewhat (favor/oppose)?

	combined	
Strongly favor	42	
Somewhat favor	27	69
Somewhat oppose	9	
Strongly oppose	18	27
DK	4	

Pre-amble for B4-B6. Collecting dues from sovereign nations is difficult and may never work very well. There are ways that the UN could become less dependent on dues. Let's look at these.

B4. Do you favor or oppose a tax on some forms of international pollution, such as ocean dumping of toxic wastes? [IF FAVOR OR OPPOSE] Is that strongly or somewhat (favor/oppose)?

	combined	
Strongly favor	65	
Somewhat favor	16	82
Somewhat oppose	4	
Strongly oppose	12	16
DK	3	

B5. Do you favor or oppose a tax on some forms of international pollution, such as carbon emissions by each country's power plants, cars, and industries?
[IF FAVOR OR OPPOSE] Is that strongly or somewhat (favor/oppose)?

	combined	
Strongly favor	51	
Somewhat favor	28	79
Somewhat oppose	8	
Strongly oppose	10	18
DK	3	

B6. Do you favor or oppose a world-wide tax on international financial trading in currencies?
[IF FAVOR OR OPPOSE] Is that strongly or somewhat (favor/oppose)?

	combined	
Strongly favor	19	
Somewhat favor	26	45
Somewhat oppose	20	
Strongly oppose	22	41
DK	14	

E7. Do you favor or oppose allowing member states to purchase a kind of national security insurance. In return for paying the UN an annual premium, UN peacekeeping forces would come to their aid if they were ever invaded by their neighbors. Premiums would be tailored to risk -- very high for excessively aggressive or militaristic nations and low for low-risk, peaceful nations. The premiums could be a bargain for many countries who live in fear of some of their neighbors and otherwise would have to spend more on defense than they would like to. All the premiums could add up to enough to fund the necessary UN peacekeeping forces and maybe even have money left over to pay for other UN operations as well as peacekeeping. Do you favor or oppose this idea for national security insurance?
[IF FAVOR OR OPPOSE] Is that strongly or somewhat (favor/oppose)?

		combined
Strongly favor	29	
Somewhat favor	33	**62**
Somewhat oppose	12	
Strongly oppose	21	**33**
DK	5	

Analysis of A1-A3, B4-B6, and E7.

E7 is a good example of a tightly worded question (138 words) describing a proposal that was earlier presented to the world in a 44 page, 16,526 word, document endorsed by many world figures, including Nobel Laureates. Of course, E7 cannot cover all the important points of a well-written document over 100 times longer, but it does get out the key ideas.

In each of the long form descriptions of the three proposals, **A1-A3**, the last sentence before, "Do you favor. . . ." gives an argument against the proposal, and from the point of view of Mitofsky's editorial in the NY Times, which explains the position endorsed by mainstream commercial pollsters (see Chapter 8, pp. 78-79, discussion of Perot campaigns) that these are balanced, unbiased questions. The contra-argument in **A3** is weak, only because nobody on the ATI survey design team at that time came up with a stronger argument.

Compare **A3** with **B6**, two questions testing support for a currency tax. The 144 word version **A3** achieves 69% support and has only 4% DKs, while the 14 word version **B6** has only 45% support and a much larger 14% DK. The short version is clearly too short and inadequate, while the long one is about as short as a version can be and still adequate to capture the public's preference.

Discontinuances. Experience in question design and survey completion shows that discontinuances (respondents hanging up on the interviewer) which can be reduced by special and expensive techniques, normally run about 40 to 50% of those respondents meeting qualifications such as adult over 18, and occur mainly at the beginning of the interview, near the point when the social contract is tacitly made. The rare discontinuances thereafter are not significantly associated with question length.

Internal Consistency Further evidence that the support for detailed proposals may be reliably captured by carefully worded questions comes from the internal consistency of such support from sample to sample and from survey to survey, by testing the effects of wording variations and pro and con argument evaluations (the debate format, described on pp. 40-42 of Chapter 4).

The responses to two questions, **A8-A9** from ATI#25, illustrate how good polling can come at the above four proposals **A1-A3** and **E7** in different ways to show internal consistency. (Four different proposals **B4-6** and **E7** were similarly tested of the **B** half sample.) The two half samples were asked of the four proposals for funding the United Nations, which they liked best and which least. The results confirmed the previous findings. Best liked in the **A** sample were the arms sales tax at 36% and in the **B** sample, pollution taxes at 53%. The most impressive result of these questions was that after each of the four proposals were presented in random order, as follows:

A: Arms sales tax, Air travel tax, Currency trading tax, UN Security Insurance Plan
B: Pollution taxes: Coal, oil and gas, Pollution taxes: ocean dumping, Currency trading tax, UN
   security insurance plan.

respondents were asked "Or just the current dues system". At a time when Senator Jesse Helms assured the world that the US opposed UN funding by any means other than direct contributions from member nations, only 10% in the **A** and 14% in the **B** sample agreed that the last-asked "just the current dues system" was best. Helms was totally off the mark.

Chapter 10. Fair and Foul Use – Taglines and Authorities

Taglines in Polls

Survey research shows that there are a very small number, really only a handful of people who are known by name to more than 80% of the general public. A few icons in entertainment, sports, government, and business are in this select circle. Even fewer stay in the circle for more than a decade. If you were designing a questionnaire and wanted to get the public's take on any of these people, good practice tells you to include a tagline that identifies the person beyond his/her name itself. Let's illustrate:

A question we mentioned at the opening of Chapter 8, p. 69,

"Do you like or dislike Bill Gates?"

could be wasted if 20% of the public, when asked this question out-of-the-blue, were confused or doubtful about who that what's-his-name fellow is. After all, Bob Gates was head of the CIA under President Bush the first, and most people have heard of dozens of Bills and Bobs and Gates'. So it is no surprise that the tagline, "Chairman of Microsoft" in:

"Do you like or dislike Bill Gates, Chairman of Microsoft?"

reduces the confusion and shrinks the doubtful group among respondents. The desired drop in DKs that follows proves that including the tagline is worthwhile.

We are dealing with the richest man in the world, in the news daily, transforming the economy, admired, hated, loved and feared. If he needs a tagline in survey research -- everyone else does too.

Sometimes the tagline is so clear and powerful that it carries most of the burden of producing a valid question response. In three Y2K surveys in 1998-9 questions were asked about who should get the blame if failure of computer chips to handle dates beginning after 1/1/00 proved to be a big national disaster, as most people in mid 1999 thought quite possible. Some questions were asked about the responsibility and accountability for such a disaster of both particular groups and key individuals. The latter included "President Clinton," "Vice President Al Gore," and "Bill Gates, president of

Microsoft." The taglines for Clinton and Gore were brief but adequate. When going down the list a new name appeared, John Koskinen, it would have been a joke not to include his tagline, "the White House Y2K Czar". That position was known well-enough to conclude from the response percentages that there was more salience for blaming Clinton and Gore than for blaming what's-his-name, yeah – that fellow, John Koskinen.

When many years ago "engine" Charlie Wilson, President of General Motors, said, "What's good for General Motors is good for the country," it caused an uproar. But the sentence you just read was strengthened by containing the nickname, the name, and the tagline, and if you were then asked your opinion about what he said, there would be no doubt about whom we were talking.

Taglines Identify and Media Establishes Authorities in Polls
Taglines play another role in political survey questions by leading us to pin down who the "authority figures" are. If you are familiar with news and current affairs interview shows on radio and TV, you know the drill. When they want expertise, talk-show hosts go for the highest ranking officials or issue-experts they can get. The top shows like PBS Newshour and Larry King Live can get just about anybody they want. They are not going to call in the Secretary of Labor when the issue is national security. But they do have some choices with that issue. Do they want the Chairman of the Joint Chiefs, the President's National Security Advisor, or the President himself? The answer is whichever official is the most knowledgeable and most recognized and trusted by the public in that issue at that time. If you watch these shows night after night, you can begin to see inside the heads of the show's hosts and producers as to how they answer that question.

The Public's Take on Authority Figures
We saw in Chapter 6, pp. 59-60, when policies on major national security issues were tested that President Bill Clinton, notoriously inexperienced by background on national security matters, was upstaged a bit by Colin Powell, the most admired general since Eisenhower. The relevant questions, both with and without the authority figures named, showed that Powell's authority was slightly higher than the President's, but not much. Pose an issue area and pundits are pretty accurate in coming up with the name and "authority" ranking of the top national authority figures on that issue.

–Ch. 10–

Group Authorities

Authority figures need not be individuals. They can be groups of leaders and experts. The Pentagon sized its demands for funding from 1993 to 2001 based on a "Two War" policy stating that, "The US should be prepared to fight two regional wars, each the size of the Gulf War, perhaps on opposite sides of the world, and win them at nearly the same time and without the help of allies." In surveys it was determined that full acceptance of each tenet of the Policy found only 7.4% in favor of meeting the requirements of all of them together. Only this tiny minority of Americans fully and completely supported the Policy. Support would increase if any of the required provisions were softened or omitted: (1) two wars (not just one); (2) each the size of the Gulf War; (3) on opposite sides of the world; (4) win them at nearly the same time; and (5) win them without the help of allies. Some versions of the two war policy that do not abandon any of these requirements, but soften them a bit can eke out 51% support for the policy, but only when a huge weight of authority is included in the question, "Our leaders, both Democrats and Republicans" favor the Policy. That is close to the all-encompassing authoritative group.

Unnamed Authorities

Authority figures need not have names. Unnamed experts may be invoked. Suppose we want to ascertain the degree of support for a policy using one of the better scales, discussed in Chapter 8, such as minus three to plus three, where zero is neutral, minus three is very opposed and plus three is very favorable. As explained in **The Debate Format**, p. 38-39, ATI uses a balanced team of issue experts to develop the debate for testing a policy by gathering and constructing pro and con arguments for and against the policy. It is often irrelevant and confusing to name the actual experts who came up with these pro and con arguments. Usually the amount of involvement varies among different team members. Generic, nameless experts suffice, and their arguments may be presented in a balanced fashion like this: [pro] "Some *experts* say . . ." [con] "Other *experts* say . . ."

There is an unbiased neutrality to introducing the arguments by "some experts" vs. "other experts". Similar impartiality is achieved by "some people" vs. "other people" and is as acceptable in most questions.

Biasing Authorities Creates BIG TIME Spin

If you find a question where balanced authority figures are replaced by authorities who are described in a biased way, like this:

"Some misled/ uninformed/ well-meaning people" on one side
vs.
"Knowledgeable people/ good Democrats/ good Republicans" on the other side

you have come upon BIG TIME spin.

Unbalanced Authorities Create Spin

The role of authority figures in affecting public support for policy up to this point has largely been restricted to authorities behind alternative policy choices of large and more-or-less equal stature. It has been useful to see the fairly fine distinctions that the public can make in this case, generally as well-considered as the distinctions of talk show producers considering who to invite on their shows. However, if we consider a large imbalance of authorities on one side of an issue, the results are very different. A heavy load of authorities all on one side can completely upset the outcome of the public's policy preference. A good example was the "Two War" policy mentioned above that has been supported by "our leaders both Republicans and Democrats" for the decade of the '90s. If the authorities truly line up, as here in an unbalanced way, the findings may or may not be spun, but not by improperly unbalanced authority figures.

Authorities Effects on Election Outcomes

Authority figures play a large role in our democracy at election time. The biggest effect comes not from the top national authority figures, but from the far greater number of local people who are respected either on the issues or for making recommendations on choosing candidates. Most important for influencing elections, these local authority figures are trusted by those people who know them and have a personal relationship with them. The personal relationships of hundreds of thousands of local authority figures outweigh the impact of authorities' with nationally recognized expertise.

How a President Can Become the Top Authority on Any Issue

George W. Bush found himself in the office of President somewhat lacking in experience and credible expertise on national issues. He had a dilemma. How was he going to be thought of as the leader he claimed to be unless he was also the top authority figure for the pressing issues?

All Presidents are confronted with tough issues continuously. In his first few months in office, Bush confined his statements to generalities and guiding principles that, lacking specifics, often left a trail of confusion as to what really were his policy positions going to turn out to be. Bush quickly set up a team consisting of authority figures in their own right: Vice President Cheney, cabinet officers and agency heads who interpreted Bush's statements for the media.

The Cheney team became the spokesmen who clarified and specified what Bush policies were, normally with a disclaimer that they were only giving their own personal interpretations or opinions. However, the words that team members were permitted to use were chosen by a special task force whose output was approved by Bush. This allowed Bush the flexibility to test ideas and to reach an understanding of the best way to present his proposals and initiatives, when in fact the input and preliminary culling and shaping of ideas was primarily done by the coordinated team and the task force. In this way Bush did come to be considered the authority figure by the media and most of the public on any issue at least for as long as this approach worked.

Since at any time team members opinions of what Bush planned to do could be dismissed with no onus falling upon himself, whenever Bush chose to do so, team member opinions were indeed over-ridden. Bush changed course risk-free, while the brunt fell upon subordinates. When all team and task force members have been shielded by the pretence that their spontaneous utterances were their own while they in fact often knew both the orchestration and the substance of Bush's decisions, then the appropriate characterization of Bush policy needs to be considered something stronger than "misleading". The word *lying* serves well. It is stronger than "self-serving interpretation" which is spin. An alternative title for this book was "Spot the Spin – and the Lie."

Chapter 11   Good Polls, Good Pollsters, Good Sponsors

Good sponsors must take responsibility for hiring good pollsters and conducting good polls. But how does a sponsor become a good sponsor and how can a good sponsor convince the public audiences for its polls that its poll findings can be trusted? This book has given many tips on how to spot the spin in polls and more generally what, besides the absence of spin, is needed to make a good poll. But what does a sponsor that wishes to produce high quality political polls have to do to be judged of top quality and how can it demonstrate that it is aspiring to do something that is much larger and more difficult than current commercial level polling. Such a sponsor is obligated to demonstrate that it is trustworthy and that sponsor may have to go to great lengths to succeed. Let's look at some of the things that a public-interest polling sponsor could do to help convince others it is performing at a high-standard level.

A Public-interest Polling Sponsor's Obligations

Primary Purpose Public-interest polling has been defined as political polling where the sponsor's primary intention is to uncover as reliably and stably as possible what the public most wants for governance. The sponsor is presumed competent and sincere. It matters little if the sponsor has other desires, hopes, or intentions for surveys, as long as all decisions as to the design, conduct, analysis, promotion and distribution of the findings, give the highest priority to finding the public's wants for governance. Uncovering the "public-interest" has to be the *primary* purpose with priority over all other purposes.

Credibility and **Trustworthiness**. It is up to the sponsoring organization(s) to establish a relationship with the audiences for its polls to persuade them of its true intentions and thus to demonstrate that it is a credible public-interest polling organization. This can be done in many ways. ATI has used the following ways in varying degrees. It is hard to see why anyone sincerely wishing to be a public-interest poll sponsor would not be pleased to follow most, if not all of them and, where practical, even strengthen them.

1. The methods used to perform the surveys should conform as a minimum to the highest generally accepted commercial polling standards.

2. Limitations of the methods used should be acknowledged frankly and fully while efforts should be made to remove or overcome significant limitations.

3. The survey and question design should be carried out by a team that includes experts in political polling and in the issue area(s) under investigation representing a wide range of viewpoints across the political spectrum. They should include some with knowledge of, or easy access to, the enormous range of policy proposals available from the government, political leaders, policy organizations, and others. The process of designing, conducting, and analyzing the survey data should be considered a collaboration between experts and the public. The important and amazing results of public-interest polling will not be achieved without both the experts fulfilling their assigned role *and* the public making its judgments. An important duty of the team is to create questions that are fair, balanced, and accurate, as defined in *Locating Consensus for Democracy,* pp. 350-353.

4. One of the most important functions of the team is seeking, culling, and refining for inclusion in the surveys a wide range of policy choice options. This is an absolutely essential feature of public-interest polling. If the choices offered are only those that leading politicians and the major news media poll on, it cannot be public-interest polling. To the extent that the survey team does not fairly and fully carry out its role, the full benefits of public-interest polling will not be realized.

5. Every member of the team should sign off on the survey report, should be recognized for his/her role in the report, and if team members disagree with any finding, those members' views should be welcomed, acknowledged, and carried in some section of the report.

6. The sponsor should make clear in its written materials, particularly in each survey report, what its intentions are. It should make plausible why it wishes to conduct surveys in issues and subjects it has chosen. It should explain how it is financed, and how it intends to use the resulting information. All results, including the full and complete wording of the interviewers' script and its own analysis, should be made public shortly after the results are available. If the sponsor can state that it does not conduct special interest polling as well, that will add to the sponsor's credibility.

7. The sponsor should be open to cooperating with any other public-interest polling organization by a willingness to share data and methodology used so that others can confirm, build on, or find limitations to the sponsor's findings.

8. The sponsor, as long as it remains an active public-interest polling organization, should encourage members of the public with unusual interests in the issues it surveys to become involved. Because they are leaders, pundits, or experts, or have had considerable practical or theoretical experience in the issue or because the issue impinges on them more than on others, such people should be invited to submit new versions of policy proposals or previously untested proposal arguments, both pro and con, for testing public support as soon as such can be scheduled into the sponsor's ongoing survey research program. If there is any charge at all for such inclusion, it should not exceed a fair allocation of the survey's full costs. The sponsor should be open to including questions in upcoming surveys that others challenge them to include.

9. Individuals who are key in the sponsoring organizations or are themselves sponsors should make clear their own biases on the policy questions in each survey by saying honestly how they would respond to these questions. Sponsors should voluntarily take the test that they ask others to voluntarily take!

10. The sponsor(s) must take responsibility for managing the design team, especially the pollsters, to make sure that those of the preceding items that the sponsor claims to be following actually are being followed.

If a sponsor conforms to these, or to most of these, suggestions, I believe that its credibility as a bona fide public-interest polling organization will be quite readily established and will increase as long as it continues to abide by these suggestions. Then others who claim to poll in the public's interest would not be able to successfully fake it for very long.

Chapter 12. Historical Persistence of Public Opinion

Public support for a government policy is *persistent*, meaning that it changes very slowly over the years -- unless a major event relevant to the issue occurs, in which case support generally shifts, if at all, in the expected direction. Moreover, when such a shift occurs for the public as a whole a parallel shift prevails for each major demographic sector except, perhaps, in the rare case that the policy is aimed at affecting a particular sector.

A related phenomenon, called *historical persistence*, can extend over decades, when new and old events occur that have features and aspects with considerable similarity. The reward for those with some understanding of the complex socio-econo-political relationship between the elites and the people and who also start to study historical public opinion will be a growing ability to predict from the old events much of what will happen as the new events begin to unfold. It is easier to understand the amazing significance of such findings by exploring case studies rather than seeking theory, starting with the first of three examples:

The All-Time *Persistence* Record – 68 Years.

Scientific polling started when George Gallup, Sr. predicted with startling accuracy the 1936 re-election of Franklin Delano Roosevelt (FDR). Other highly regarded polls showed FDR losing to the Republican candidate, Alf Landon. Gallup developed a random sample method based on sampling theory, well known to statisticians. Gallup's success in predicting the re-election of FDR in 1936 opened the modern era of polling, which soon discredited "straw" or self-selected polls that had been around since the 19th century. Gallup's methodology, as refined, is the only application of the scientific method in all of so-called "political *science*". (Please don't say that to a political science professor. He might break into tears.)

The story that spans the 68 year old era of scientific polling links President Franklin Delano Roosevelt (FDR) to current President George W. Bush. The link appears in polling data comparing public support for FDR prior to and after the attack on Pearl Harbor with support for George W Bush before and after the events of Sept 11th. No other events of modern times can be compared with either of these two, but they can be compared with each other. The eras were very different. So were many aspects of the events themselves. One of the similarities, not previously noticed, is that public support levels and trends over time, for the two leaders prove to be uncannily similar. Another similarity is that the early pollsters, like Gallup and Roper, did surveys that explored the public's interest, while only in the last few years has the importance of public-interest polling started to be realized again. Five years ago, one of George Gallup Sr.'s associates back in the '60s, Winston (Wink) Franklin, wrote "Gallup was a true believer in public-interest polling and would be appalled if he could see how opinion polling is used today". Polling indeed has become an industry dominated by commercial pollsters, including today's huge Gallup and Roper organizations, catering to moneyed special interests. A tide of high priced pollsters, campaign managers, political advisors, pundits and media overwhelmed the earlier political landscape of FDR's era.

Bush's job approval rating by the public before 9/11 hovered in the range 55% to 62% for the eight prior months of his presidency. Over many years my colleagues and I conducted public interest polls examining why and when the U.S. public favors the use of force. An unexpected attack on the U.S. homeland our data showed would produce nearly unanimous support for action against the perpetrators. In the case of 9/11 the required action had to be a global effort to track down and bring to justice those responsible.

Immediately after 9/11 Bush's ratings shot up. Within a few weeks Bush had made clear he was pursuing a course very close to what most people wanted. His rating peaked at 90%. For the year thereafter it remained high, but slowly drifted down, crossing 66% August 2002.

Bush's high ratings enabled him to get from Congress almost whatever he wanted. High presidential approval ratings in war-time also squelch alternatives to the president's *domestic* legislative and regulatory initiatives. Declaring war gave Bush an opportunity to push his domestic agenda successfully.

How do FDR's approval ratings compare with Bush's? In his second term, well before the start of WW II in Europe, FDR's approval ratings were within the same range as Bush's, as follows:

Roper/Fortune: May 1938, 55%;

Gallup: 1937: Nov., 63%;   1938: May, 54%;   July, 52%;   Sep., 52%.

An important part of this story is the opportunity for discovery that drove the initiators of the era of scientific polling. Polling was so new that experimenting and learning from survey to survey occurred at every opportunity. Tests on the effects of different question wordings were routine. Gallup and Roper found that many small changes in wording and formatting made almost no difference in the responses to poll questions, but some did. Here is an example that is important for our Bush/FDR comparison. Before Sept. 1938 Gallup's wording of the rating question was crude, "Are you for or against Roosevelt today?" After Sep. 1938, Gallup switched to what was proving to be a more standard "approve/ disapprove" wording that from Nov. 1938 thru July 1940 produced approval for FDR in a narrow 56%-64% band. Dips down to 52% no longer occurred. So, for *similar question wording* Bush's approval band, 55%-62%, before 9/11was virtually the same as Roosevelt's 56%-64% before 12/7/41.

After Dec. 7th, 1941, it was war time. Gallup ran surveys once or twice a month. Roper specialized in questions on approval of Roosevelt's attitude toward specific issues and legislation. Looking closely at the evolution of their question design and wording, it is clear that both were seeking reliability and consistency of responses with reasonable concern with the fairness, balance, and accuracy of their findings.

The early pollsters felt free to make occasional word substitutions to create new questions. For example, along with the standard "Do you approve or disapprove today of Roosevelt as President", in March 1940, Gallup asked a question never before tried, "Do you approve or disapprove of the way Mrs. Roosevelt has conducted herself as First Lady?" Eleanor received a 68% approval rating, 8 points higher than Franklin's 60%. The "First Lady" question was never asked again. Today commercial pollsters, as we noted in

Chapter 2, would consider such questions irrelevant for their purposes, which are to tailor question wording and formatting to maximize public support for the policies that best satisfy their client's financial backers.

For the first year of the war, Gallup surveys showed support for the way FDR was handling his job, as follows: Jan. '42 over 85% approval, slowly dropping as follows: Feb., 82%; Mar.-May, 80%; June-Aug., 77%; Sep.-Nov., 72%. -- very similar to the high but dropping off ratings George Bush received in the three years since 9/11.

After 12/7/41, approval for FDR's handling of *domestic* issues, like his overall rating, initially very high, slowly dropped off. It is amazing that the founder of random sample polling asked this question with a phrase (see italics) that is still sometimes used today.

Gallup: "Do you approve/disapprove of President Roosevelt's policies *here at home?"*
Jan. '42, 77%   Feb. '42, 73%,   June '42, 71%

Pushing the analogy to its limit, this data from six-decade old archives suggests that for at least six months after 9/11 Bush would be successful with both international and domestic initiatives and that was correct.

On the other hand, considering specific issues and legislation, whether it was early pollsters questioning FDR's support or current pollsters questioning Bush's support, results vary widely from one issue to the next, sometimes favorable and sometimes not.

What can be done with these findings? In the last year the obvious and unique parallel between the 9/11/01 and 12/7/41 attacks was noted by many people, but did anyone think to look into polling databases during the year to get an insight into how Bush's ratings might unfold? To my knowledge, no.

Having written about the stability and persistence of public-interest poll findings, still I too was surprised to find both the size and trends in public support for both the president's domestic and international policies would be so consistent over a 60 year period. Though relatively few, there are still enough public-interest polls conducted now to be compared with those few of 60 years ago, demonstrating an uncanny similarity between public opinion levels and shifts during the old era and the new when the circumstances are sufficiently similar for the two as we have seen comparing the Roosevelt era with the Bush era. The stability of public opinion when unusual conditions repeat themselves is worth examining and may continue to prove awesome.

Second Example: **"How much of the time do you trust the government in Washington to do what's right?"**

This question, word-for-word, has been asked annually for 46 years — often much more frequently than that. Respondents are asked to choose one of three responses:
1. "Just about always," 2. "Most of the time," or 3. "Only some of the time".

The findings show a long-term trend of increasing mistrust, leading us to label this the "mistrust" question. Starting at a low of 22-23% in the years 1958-1965, "only some of the time" climbed to a high plateau of about 79% during '93-'97. The all-time high was 82% in November 1993. Over the years '58-'97, "most of the time" dropped from about 60% to 15%. Support for "just about always" has been in the single digits — negligible — during the 30-year period of 1967-1997.

This growth of mistrust was by no means linear or smooth. During times of government scandals from Watergate to Whitewater, mistrust increased much more rapidly than the long-term trend line. The easiest way to understand the phenomenon is to know that mistrust resulting from major scandals peters out in a few years — not down to where it was before the scandal broke, but about half way down. Noticing this from years of survey research has yielded a public-interest polling rule of thumb, "It takes about twice the amount of good happening to produce as much increase in trust as the amount of bad to cause loss of trust." Though crude and simplistic, the belief, "Once bitten, twice shy", seems to characterize the public view.

In the eight-year period following — June 1993 to March 2001 — the mistrust trend line decreased slowly from 79% to 69%. The trend line is the best-fitting straight line for the mistrust question data points available from the largest polling database repository. A dozen well-respected polling organizations, most asking the question repeatedly in a series of surveys, had asked the mistrust question 42 times in that period. March 2001 was the date of the last asking prior to the event that changed the world, Sept. 11, 2001. After being asked almost monthly for the previous three years, it is odd that the mistrust question was not asked by any pollster in the six months period from March 2001 until two weeks after Sept. 11, when the Washington Post found mistrust had dropped enormously, down to 36%.

During September-December 2001, the mistrust question was asked four more times, producing "only some of the time" support bouncing up and down a lot in the range of 31% to 53%. In view of the anthrax scares that occurred then, on top of the roller-coaster aftermath of 9/11, this rapid fluctuation was not surprising. The 31% low is 38 points below the 69% low of the trend line. For understanding public opinion under stressful conditions, these findings are very significant. Look at it this way.

After Sept. 11, for the first and only time in the 45-year history of the mistrust question, mistrust plummeted and trust in government rapidly rose for reasons having little to do with government scandals. The explanation that best fits the facts is a new public-interest poll finding, apparently previously unnoticed. When the homeland is as seriously threatened as it was then, about one-third of Americans who — if asked — would have previously expressed their mistrust in government, were now ready to turn around and trust the government. Seemingly independent of any improvement in its performance, government was seen as the only force realistically imaginable that could help the United States overcome such a traumatic setback.

From Feb. 2002 through Oct 2003, the mistrust question has been asked in polls another 12 times. Mistrust rose sharply after June 2002, up to 61%, when the United States government began focusing on Iraq. Many thought an Iraq invasion only tenuously and indirectly concerned homeland security. Mistrust after June was half-way back to its all time high, and more than two-thirds back to its early 2001, pre-Sept. 11 levels. It is reasonable to reduce the public's new attitude that "Mistrust is back" to "Government? -- what's it done for us lately?"

A new, severe and successful al Qaeda attack on U.S. soil might quickly boost trust in government to the levels reached for the three months after Sept. 11. That would be a big boost in public support for President George W. Bush. What's good for al Qaeda turns out to be good for Bush.

It is already known that the relationship works in reverse. The very nature of terrorism does not discriminate between ordinary, innocent people and elites. To al Quaeda, the "innocents" are seen to be less innocent the more they support their president. If public support for Bush rises, al Qaeda, at least in the Muslim world can increasingly justify its terrorist acts. Does this two-way relationship seem weird? Psychiatrists call it "co-dependency." There are other government reform findings that support such types of co-dependence.

The larger picture that emerges from a study of these findings is that responses in public-interest polls have a persistency not unlike a country's culture itself. A culture resists change. It tends to fend off novel challenges — new art, music, status attitudes, food acceptance, etc. When new developments are persistent and strong enough, aspects of culture do change, but only as little as necessary to keep most people reassured. Close study can uncover and identify these developments and their underlying factors.

This example illustrates that the persistence, resistance to change, and flipping as little as possible also characterize the long-term morphing of attitudes revealed by good public-interest polls.

Third Example: **Gulf War, 1990-91, Lessons for Further Middle-East Invasions.** During and shortly after the Gulf War my colleagues and I conducted four surveys that may now tell us something about how public attitudes will unfold in the course of an accelerating confrontation with Iraq leadership or lack thereof. One important difference is that in the first Gulf War the issue was oil -- not weapons of mass destruction, not regime change, not finding al Qaeda, not making Iraq into a model democracy. Many, looking at the oil interests that permeate the Bush2 administration, believe that the issue is still oil. So far, the mainstream press only carries that linkage incidentally, as in cartoons.

The US Secretary of State, James Baker, in 1990 explained to the troops sitting in the Arabian desert and facing war, that their purpose was protecting "jobs, jobs, jobs". The administration of President George Bush, Sr., presented publicly no high-minded objective like "bringing democracy to the Middle East" or producing "a lasting peace in the Middle East," which 87% of the people said in ATI's survey #14 was "very" or "extremely" important as an objective of the impending war. Only more recently has a Bush president come to understand through ATI public-interest polling when the American people favor the use of force and what leaders have to do to get support for war. Bush2 has fully and masterfully adopted those ideas.

Some problems and opportunities of the two situations twelve years apart are surprisingly similar. One similarity is that during the five month US led Gulf War build-up along the Arabian-Iraq-Kuwait border, it seemed that the only thing that would stop the US invasion of Iraq would be Iraq's prior capitulation. A question asked at that time was introduced with this lead-in:

"Here are some things that some people thought we should have done but did not do before the situation in the Persian Gulf happened. As I mention each one, please tell me if you think it would have helped a lot, helped a little, or not helped at all, to make the confrontation with Iraq unnecessary" . . . .

The question then went on to present nine things that were not done, six of which got 70+% consensus support for helping "at least a little" and all nine had majority support. Here are the responses in rank order of "helped a lot":

	Helped a lot
1st. Supported increased research and development of energy sources other than oil	59%
2nd. Waged a campaign to increase energy efficiency and conservation in autos, homes, offices, and factories	51%
3rd. Given more incentives to oil companies for exploration and recovery operations in places outside the Middle East	47%

4th.	Strengthened the UN peace keeping capabilities		47%

4th. Strengthened the UN peace keeping capabilities   47%
5th. Further increased our government strategic oil reserves   46%
6th. Continued the mandatory annual improvement in miles per
        gallon of US autos discontinued in 1984   41%
7th. Not aided Iraq in the 8-year Iran—Iraq war just ended   33%
8th. Put a tax on foreign oil of 5 cents per gallon more each year
        for ten years, totaling 50 cents at the end of ten years   19%
9th. Supported Israel less and the Arab nations more   17%

Talk about issues where the people differ from their leaders, look at the four that ranked 1st, 2nd, 3rd and 6th! How long before any US leader wanted to give those ideas any mention? It was seven long years later that President Clinton began to offer such proposals. When ATI asked for the one thing that would have helped the most from among these nine proposals, the 1st still topped the list, but the 7th came in second. Many people, not thinking about the fact that the United States had aided Iraq in the Iran-Iraq war, until reminded in this question set, boosted that item up to second place in importance.

While questions like these are very revealing, some may be very misleading when taken out of context or not examined closely. We close with an inadvertently misleading question illustrating this point, asked in Oct. '87, three years before the Gulf War, with lead-in (i.e., frame):

> "I'm going to read the names of the countries that are thought to
> have a nuclear capability. After I read the list, please tell me which
> one or two of these countries gives you the greatest concern – I
> mean which ONE OR TWO you feel would be the most likely to
> explode a nuclear weapon" . . .

Notice how "Iraq" topped the percent mentions list, far above all others:

Iraq	64%	United States	7%
Soviet Union	36%	France	3%
Israel	18%	Britain	1%
China	16%	Others/	
India	9%	DK	10%

Note that neither Iran nor any other Arab or Muslim country was included in the list offered. Such additional offerings would have detracted from Iraq mentions, probably substantially. We simply don't know if Iraq would have dropped from first place.

Please do not use this question as an example of any mystical prognosticative ability of the people. There is some wisdom among "the people" that emerges when asking what people want for policy and legislation. It does not emerge in questions asking the people to make predictions. Public-interest polling shows from many examples that the public is no better at prediction than the experts. Neither is very good.

Beyond the Three Historical Persistence Examples. There are other historical events that have stimulated survey findings worth studying. Included are those end-of-an-era questions that the mainstream pollsters dismiss such as Kathy Frankovic, head of CBS polling, who told us in Chapter 2, CBS does not do "social research". *Locating Consensus for Democracy* explored public opinion on why the Soviet union collapsed, why it collapsed when it did and not sometime earlier or later (pages 66-69), what lessons the US learned from the war in Vietnam (p. 108), and similar end-of-era questions. It is important for the elite to understand public reactions, opinions, and attitudes that have built up over the long years that mark an era. Those who do not learn from history are destined to repeat old mistakes.

Chapter 13. Good Polling to Keep Democracy Alive and Elections Honest

In Chapter 10 we saw the utility of often including authority figures in testing support for policy. Since adequate questions tend to be lengthy, to hold respondents attention, authorities need to be identified in a few brief words. Political spinmasters would love to trick the public into elevating their client into the position of top authority in an issue area. This means that they seek to bias the brief descriptions of opposing authorities so as to favor their client. As we saw in Chapter 10, p. 92, such bias is readily observed. The resulting spin is easy to uncover.

In the political life of the US, a handful of top national officials have learned to play an aggressive power game that in recent years has become essential for rising to the ranks of the very few who control the government's agenda and who, as long as they are successful, become entrenched in powerful, self-perpetuating roles satisfying to themselves, their parties, and their financial supporters. These top officials determine what government does and accordingly have a much greater impact on the entire country than the minor game of designating authority figures in poll questions. Yet the two are related.

Public-interest polling has revealed in the past decade or so that there is a total disconnect in all major issue areas between what consensus levels (67%+) of the public with good reason want and the governance that top officials deliver. What we want is not what we get. Top officials, who themselves often conduct excellent polls, as well as those political elites who follow public polls closely seem unaware of the total disconnect. How can that be? Clues to the answer coming from public-interest polling and political developments have been analyzed, sorted, and finally put together in a clear and astounding story. Now for the first time in print this chapter reveals how top leaders of both parties have been unaware of the total disconnect and have managed to ignore it without ever being challenged by the news media or political elites. Here is the story from the beginning:

Americans Talk Issues (ATI) was organized in 1987 by me as a non-profit, public service cooperative project initially to help all candidates running for president in 1988 find out what the public wanted the new President to do on national security matters by conducting a series of bipartisan polls. The project used small balanced teams of top polling and issue experts to design and analyze the polls. The findings were widely distributed. By early 1988 an ATI team headed by Maddy Hochstein, of the Daniel Yankelovich Group, had visited all 13 campaign headquarters (7 Democrat and 6 Republican) and explained ATI's offer to all at no charge: (1) to test national security questions that the candidates might wish to have included in the surveys without publicly revealing the source of the questions, (2) to give the campaigns private briefings on survey results as requested and (3) to release the results of each survey to the campaigns before the public release. Through an advisor that was the contact person with the ATI project, twelve candidates submitted questions. The lone exception, Mike Dukakis, was a little surprising since Mike's pollster, Marttila and Kiley, was ATI's Democratic pollster. To facilitate confidentiality the questions went only to Maddy and to me. I kept my copies in a secure place to prevent leaks. When the campaigns were well underway and most of the candidates' questions had already been covered in the briefings, I took out my confidential copy of the candidates' original questions.

Sitting alone, I carefully studied them. They covered many topics from all different points of view, not unlike the ATI surveys themselves. But something more important became very clear. Clearly without any contact between themselves, the candidates' advisors had asked ATI to find out in effect if the public believed what the candidates were saying. Did the public agree with the national security statements and positions that were then coming out publicly in their own speeches and releases? This was not what the ATI surveys supposed to be for. As mentioned above, the ATI surveys were designed and the question wording developed to ask the people what they wanted the next president *to do*; they were "what-to-do" questions. The candidates' questions were all bent on asking how should the candidates best express publicly their own convictions on issues. They were questions on "what-to-say" to get elected, not "what-to-do" if elected. I was beginning to understand that the different purposes of the two kinds of questions lead to very different survey designs and findings, and if the surveys were properly conducted, the "what-to-do" public-interest polling surveys showed a public view that was persistent, internally consistent, and resistant to change by counter-arguments. It was understandable that candidates would mis-use this opportunity, but it made me sad to think that the candidates wanted to get confirmation that their positions were acceptable to the voters rather than finding what the voters themselves wanted. The same pattern was pretty much repeated in the '92 election.

Going into campaign behavior a little more deeply was something I noted without fully understanding until many years later its significance. Each candidate's advisor asked mainly questions about the policy proposals being tested in speeches by the *other* candidates, not their own. It took me many more years of survey research to fully understand that the reason for that was that each candidate pretty much knew what policies and governance approaches they were going to use if elected, yes, primarily the policies that their financial backers desired, whether explained through lobbyists or in person.

By the time of the '96 election ATI had discovered something new: campaign pollsters familiar with the art and science of survey and question design, if they polled enough, if they covered an issue from various points of view and studied the effect of question wording variations, would eventually find from "what-to-say" polls pretty much what you could find more accurately, completely, convincingly and quickly from surveys oriented around "what-to-do", which by '92 we had dubbed "public-interest polling."

Beginning after the '94 election, these effects were starting to be found by campaign pollsters working for real candidates. Let's start with the Bill Clinton story.

In his book, *"Behind the Oval Office,"* pollster Dick Morris, explained how he designed and conducted a program that played a significant role in re-electing President Clinton in 1996. Morris convinced Clinton that the program would get him re-elected and for that goal Clinton was ready to do almost anything. The program required testing public support for hundreds of new policy proposals that Clinton himself liked. Morris gathered these proposals one-on-one from Clinton and his cabinet level advisors during a period of about a year. The program required sequential media blitzing of one major metropolitan area after another (excluding Washington, New

York, and Los Angeles where the political media and the Republicans were concentrated and might awaken the Republicans to start an early counter-program of their own). Prior to each blitz, Morris conducted quiet polling within each metropolitan area, found one or more proposals that were strongly supported (usually 75%+) by the local public, and from these, with Clinton's help, chose one. The heart of the blitz was a TV spot of Clinton explaining and promoting the chosen proposal that he and Morris already knew, the public really liked.

The ultimate cost of the program was $85 million, largely spent on the TV spots and other media promotion. After each metropolitan area blitz, Morris again polled to show the President's popularity generally rising slightly in the area – Morris took note of increases as small as 1%. As the program continued, the cumulative effect boosted Clinton's nationwide approval rating into the 50-60% range, quite high for a President beleaguered by growing scandals.

Clinton had decided that selling White House access was the only way he could raise the enormous amount of money the program demanded. Presidents had been selling access for years but never on such a large scale.

Republican accusations, amplified by the mainstream news media, started an avalanche of scandals that dogged Clinton's second term – initially selling Lincoln bedroom overnights and White House breakfasts/coffees to $100,000 plus campaign donors and later the Monica Lewinsky, Paula Jones, affairs, et al. The scandals led to legal challenges beginning with investigations of Clinton's involvement in Arkansas corruption, dominated by the impeachment hearings and still dogging him as he left office in 2001.

Morris' polls, which cost only a fraction of the 85 million, obtained findings that accurately showed what the public wanted in the many issue areas they touched on. They fall under the heading of **Governance Advice** discussed on pp.58-61 of *Locating Consensus for Democracy*, where it explains why it is fair to label such polls as "public-interest polls". One caveat – I have not seen the precise wording of the questionnaires and so cannot make as definitive judgment as I otherwise would. Morris, like many in Washington, has low ethical standards, as evidenced by: (1) His foolish, adolescent affair with a prostitute that forced Clinton to drop him as pollster for a time and brought Morris lots of personal and marital trouble, (2) His total acceptance of polling on the Internet, described in his book *"VOTE.COM"*, without once mentioning the main problem, not yet fully resolved, on using the Internet for surveys: how to obtain a credible unbiased sample of all sectors of the public. A demonstration of the dominating effect of this problem is given in the section **Prodigy Example** of p.341 *Locating Consensus for Democracy*. As he was positioning himself to enter a huge potential market for polling on the Internet, Morris simply failed to mention this problem in VOTE.COM.

After the election, Andrew Kohut, a media-prominent pollster with the Pew Foundation, showed that Clinton's bump-up from the Morris' program had faded by election day. Of course, it might have faded even more if Morris' program had not happened. Clinton's ratings for doing a good job as President stayed high throughout 1994-2000, in spite of general public disgust with his fundraising methods, his womanizing, and his legalistic arguments to deflect accountability for his personal behavior. This suggests that Morris' program did have an important effect. There is no way to measure the difference between what happened and what might have happened.

A rash of new developments in polling occurred in the 2000 campaign. Let's look now at the Republican side. Fred Steeper of Market Strategies in Michigan has been ATI's Republican pollster and a member of the ATI polling design team since 1987. He was George Bush senior's pollster in both the '88 and '92 elections and was George W Bush's pollster in the 2000 campaign and presidency to date. Before the election, to distinguish him from his father whose name is very similar, Bush, the younger, was widely and affectionately known as Dubya.

Mocking his opponents, Gore and Clinton, for relying on polls to decide what to do as president, Dubya explains that, in contrast, he "makes decisions based on sound principles", not polls. In fact, he quietly and very effectively uses polls to find out when and how he should speak publicly about what he wants to do, aiming for maximum public support for his policies and actions. He does it often. Polls for his benefit were run in 2001 at levels twice what Bill Clinton spent in his first year.

Dubya told Steeper at the beginning of the campaign that polling would not be very important for him because he is a leader and does not need to ask the public what people want him to do. He knew what he would do if elected. He needed to know how to get elected by best stating his positions in ways that the public understands and appreciates. He had to sell himself and his ideas and only for that did he need polling. During the campaign Dubya conducted polls with the viewpoint of learning "What do I have to say to keep the public as happy as possible?" These are polls on what to say to get elected. When continued after the election they are essentially the same, "What do I have to say to get re-elected?"

As the campaign progressed Steeper realized that if he put together what all the public's responses in the Republican polls in each area meant he could tell W a lot about what the public wanted too. This was not unexpected. As mentioned three pages back, ATI polling team had already begun to see that. Steeper thought of a clever metaphor describing the process as "connecting the dots" in analogy with those "connect the dots" puzzles which reveal the outline of, say, an elephant only when you connect the dots by the numbers.

When gathered at poll finding briefings that Steeper conducted, neither Dubya nor any of his top advisors took notice of how to "connect the dots" and would not welcome an attempt by Steeper to do that. It would have sounded like Steeper was saying to the distinguished candidate and his advisors, "You're all wrong." Consultants who try to upstage top campaign advisors and say anything that sounds like, "You're all wrong." are usually shown the door – permanently. In contrast, we saw in Chapter 3, p. 30, that when Steeper is working for or advising public-interest pollsters, he knows very well how to do "what-should-I-do" question design and wording. Steeper gives his clients, presidents or policy mavens, what they want.

In three presidential campaigns, democrats Bill Clinton and Al Gore and in one Senatorial campaign, Hillary Clinton, never had an advisor who understood the full picture. Their leading polling advisors were in sequence, Stanley B Greenberg, Dick Morris, and Mark J. Penn. It was not until he

112   – Ch.13–

was out of office after the 2000 election did Bill and Hillary come to appreciate the value of understanding the people's wants through good polling. This does not mean that the people will benefit much, since the way that politicians will use that understanding will do more for enhancing their own careers than satisfying the public's legitimate needs.

The evidence that the thinking of Bill and Hillary Clinton has evolved in this way came from the very helpful article, "Presidency by Poll", by John F. Harris, a Post staff reporter, published on pp. 9-10 of the Jan. 8-14th 2001 issue of the Washington Post National Weekly Edition, that came out just after Dubya had become President-elect. Harris explained that since the '96 election, Clinton had become a devoted aficionado of polling, analyzing the meaning of polls like an expert. In other words, in Steeper's language Clinton was connecting the dots.

Clinton himself was following the polls of Mark J. Penn, who was originally brought in by Dick Morris to take responsibility for the polling required in Morris program that put Clinton over the top in '96. In the article, lightly edited, Harris stated:

"Clinton had fired his early pollster, Stanley Greenberg. Four current and former Clinton aides say the president told them he preferred his new pollsters, Morris and Penn, because they do not merely diagnose problems – they tell me what to do." This confirmed what I wrote on p. 402 of *Locating consensus for Democracy* that Greenberg told me six years earlier, 'I take it as a badge of honor that I never told the President what to do.' Greenberg's attitude on this point had not changed in all that time.

Despite the enormous value of his research, Harris did not recognize that the difference between the success of Penn-advised candidates who learn "what-to-do" and the failure of Greenberg-advised candidates who only learn "what-to-say" was due to these two different approaches to polling. This deficiency is best remedied I think by repeating Harris' closing conclusions, verbatim, without omissions, in *italics*, within quotation marks, and interrupted in a few places by **my comments in bold:**

"While Penn was still Gore's advisor, the two exchanged sharp words on whether 'Clinton fatigue' would be a major factor in the 2000 elections. Penn insisted the answer was no; Gore devoutly believed it was yes and fired Penn a few days later. Greenberg became a key advisor to Gore. Greenberg's devotees believe Gore found his natural voice as a candidate only when he abandoned the tepid brand of politics Penn espoused." ['tepid' is the campaign advisors way of describing doing what the public wants rather than doing what they want, a development which gets advisors very excited.   In any case, Gore fired Penn, took on Greenberg and lost the election. Most folks, right left, and center agree that Gore did not run as good a campaign as he could have. A better campaign, as well as a margin of popular support of 10%, rather than 1%, would certainly have elected him.]

"There was another candidate in 2000 who had been advised by important Democratic lobbyists and strategists to fire Penn but chose not to: Hillary Rodham Clinton.   Penn's role in her New York Senate campaign ruffled as many feathers as his White House work. All through 2000, an argument brewed between Hillary Clinton's consultants in Washington – an uneasy alliance of Penn and media consultants in Washington – and her campaign staff in New York. The New Yorkers wanted her to spend more time promoting her biography and addressing voters' doubts about her personality; Penn insisted that she talk almost exclusively about issues." [Public-interest polling has found over and over again that the public is much more concerned with what will be done on the major issues, which affect many more of them, than on items that have little or no direct effect]. *"Things got so bad, campaign aides say, that last summer the candidate angrily summoned both sides in the White House to order an end of the feuding. In the end, Hillary Clinton's 55% victory"* [compared to Gore's anemic popular vote plurality over Dubya's of 0.5%] *left Penn vindicated. Late in Clinton's term, even officials in the White House who once scorned it have become reconciled to the Morris-Penn style of politics.* [That is finding out what people really want on the issues. Even Gore probably began to rethink what he might have done better.]
"Ultimately, Penn succeeded because his notion of politics meshed perfectly with that of the president who was his patron. 'I believe strongly in Democratic activism if you do it the right way', Penn says.' The right way is

one that gets results through consensus. **[i.e. heals the disconnect].** *The wrong way is one that seeks to divide the country"* **[i.e. chooses policy without knowing or caring what the public wants.]**

One big question remains. When will a credible candidate catch on to how best to get elected President – or will they all stay stupid for many more elections? Until that happens democracy in the US will remain tenuous and corrupted.

Both Bill Clinton and George W. Bush by the turn of the century had finally understood the possibilities for using public-interest ("what-do-I-do") polling, as well as the traditional standby for presidential candidates, "what-should-I-say" polling, but there is a big difference. Clinton is out of office and Bush is aiming at a second term in 2004. What about future presidential elections? Would a competent and attractive candidate who chose to base his/her campaign on public-interest "what-do-I-do" polls walk off with the big prize? Not necessarily, as we can see from examining the electability problems of a couple of well-known former candidates.

If ever a presidential candidate had clear and popular positions on major issues, it was Ralph Nader in the 2000 campaign. Nader has immense knowledge of the bad practices of corporations, the need for environmental protection, and waste and corruption in government. His campaign consisted of making those evils known.

Nader had major weaknesses in areas beyond and outside of his policy positions. If I, a public-interest polling maven, were advising Nader on how to frame his 2000 campaign to rise above the single-digit support level, I would have recommended:

(1) Your campaign efforts should *downplay* issues. Only occasionally show your impressive grasp of issues.

(2) Most of your energy, resources and time should focus on explaining, clearly and consistently, who you are and how you would be effective in the White House. Frankly most people, including me, have trouble visualizing you being president. Making a good speech, yes. With a hostile Congress

and a Republican-leaning court system, how would you get a law of your choosing passed? And if you did, how would you get public support and compliance that could stand up against the clout of the corporations? What in your background, personality or character prepares you to handle the large range of difficult situations that will reach your desk? You would have had to address these questions directly, honestly and compellingly to be effective in raising your ratings. I don't know if you could do it. If you could, you would have risen rapidly into the double-digit support column, which was your basic intention for yourself and for the Green Party.

In January 2004 I along with many others were called by Nader, asking our opinion on whether he should run again. I strongly advised him not to, based largely on the points made in this paragraph.

Al Gore's deficiency was somewhat similar. He kept changing who he was. If he was "Mr. Environment", how come he and Bill Clinton achieved so little improvement in environmental policy in eight years? Was he a Washington insider or a good old boy from Tennessee? Did he take an easy job in the military during the Vietnam War or was he a patriot performing well the job assigned? What did his changing appearance, clothes and facial hair, mean about who he was? He failed to define himself for the public.

President George W. Bush, much less knowledgeable about many issues and less articulate, during the 2000 campaign could respond to an inquiry about his heavy drinking, without denying any allegation, yet be absolved because his response explained who he was both then and now. He said, "When I was young and foolish, I did foolish things," implying now, older and wiser, "no more foolish things." That was apparently all that the media needed to put to rest any concern for the threat of Bush recidivism in office. Bush's drinking was hardly mentioned again in the mainstream media.

Steeper's briefings of George W. Bush have been revealed in detail by the course of action Bush and his national security advisors took in preparation for the invasion of Iraq. Bush knew that well over 70% of the American people will favor using whatever force it takes to topple rogue dictators guilty of heinous crimes (limited to international terrorism/drug trafficking, acquiring weapons of mass destruction, and gross violation of human rights of his own people), *provided* these three conditions are met

1. all peaceful means to do so have failed or US troops have already been deployed

2. *and* the action has been endorsed by the UN or supported by a broad group of allies

3. *and* the war has a high-minded purpose (specifically NOT just to acquire access to oil).

Bush and his advisors learned this lesson well, but not perfectly as this incident shows: When Bush spoke to the UN General Assembly in 2002, he argued carefully, forcefully and quite persuasively for UN support for an Iraq invasion. But trying not to risk losing his base domestic supporters, those who enjoy UN bashing, he appended to his main argument the admonition that if the UN did not vote to support the US-led coalition-of-the-willing, the US would ignore the UN and the UN would become irrelevant. He was accepting the implication that doing so would violate US responsibilities to the UN, tantamount to a treaty violation in the eyes of most UN members. This action alone united most of the world in opposition to supporting the US invasion and doomed what would have been necessary to hold support for the invasion by the US public in the 80%-90% range. Holding the support of more than a bare majority of Americans will be increasingly difficult as long as the US is still in Iraq.

It is hard to believe that presidential candidates, from now on, will not also understand how to use both public-interest polling **and** "what-should-I-say" polls. It is sad that they will probably modify their positions secretly and as minimally as possible (as W has been doing) to conform to the teachings of public-interest polling while giving, as usual, top priority to financial backers' demands and betting that the public would not feel too manipulated or too ignored to furnish enough support to deliver the presidency to them.

Would any of the current Democratic presidential candidates for 2004 do this or, even better, forgo the support of big financial backers? The early frontrunner, Howard Dean, seemed to be in tune with the public's needs and wants without having particularly studied or commissioned public-interest polls, but as a medical doctor and a popular governor of a small state with successful terms as Chairman of the Organization of US Governors, both Democrats and Republicans, he was already well aware of what constituted populist positions. He found a way to finance his campaign without big backers. He was the only candidate untainted by not having sought or held a national political office. Distance from Washington insiders started as (and could have remained) the measure of "clean" in this election, where a lifetime in his father's political limelight, and after a full term as president made Bush, who never held national political office previously, now the consummate insider. Democratic primary voters, looking more to selecting the candidate that would be most likely to beat Bush, turned to Senator John Kerry, the presumptive Democratic candidate-elect, who is also certainly a Washington insider. With this two-person slate, "clean" will not mean "furthest from Washington".

In the early Democratic primary debates, many populist and progressive ideas that resonate quite well with majorities of voters emerged and, since unseating Bush has been the top challenge for all the Democratic candidates, it is not surprising that the ideas from the various candidates converged considerably during the long Democratic debate period, but could never reach total agreement. Each had to maintain at least a few distinctions for responding to the perennial question, "What distinguishes you from the other candidates?"

A good way to follow the campaign and current poll findings more generally, is to go on www.pollingreport.org which is updated almost daily, to see how goes "Bush vs. Kerry" (or whatever Democratic candidate has the party's post-convention mandate). If you do this, you will know as accurately as the big name political pundits which horse is winning the race. Have fun. Place your bets carefully. After the election, current poll findings on socio-econo-political will enrich and deepen your understanding of when and why you agree/disagree with the public.

What happened in the 2000 election will be put in context after we examine the largest state-wide election ever conducted, the California governor recall election, of 2003, which benefited by learning from the mistakes of the Florida 2000 election employing novel techniques that are little known and should be an example for state Secretary of States and county supervisors of elections in 2004.

When it was clear that a petition to recall the governor had succeeded in forcing a special election, the California courts resolved an enormous range of contentious opinions on how the special election to recall and replace Gov. Gray Davis was to be conducted.

The election would proceed with this firm schedule:

Election day: Oct. 7

Certification of the vote by Secretary of State Kevin Shelley,
     no later than: Nov. 15

If Davis was recalled, the inauguration date of the new governor: Nov. 17.

The ballot, it was agreed, was to have two parts. In Part 1, the voter was asked to vote "yes" (Gray Davis should be recalled) or "no" (he should not be). If, of those voting in Part 1, 50% or more voted "no," Davis would serve out his remaining three-year term. If the number of "no" voters in Part 1 was less than 50%, the leading candidate in Part 2 would be governor-elect. Davis was prohibited from running in Part 2. Mindful of the imperative set by this tight schedule, draconian measures were put in place: no judicial challenge of the election outcome and no request for a recount. The election could easily have turned out to be a fiasco. Everybody recognized that the votes cast to retain Davis as governor ("no" in Part 1), might well be less than 50% of the votes cast in Part 1, but still much greater than the votes cast for the leading candidate in Part 2. If public appeal were broadly distributed among the 163 candidates of Part 2, this might easily have resulted in a governor-elect whose vote total was less than 50%, possibly even less than 10%, of the votes cast for Davis in Part 1.

Though far-fetched, an even more disastrous outcome would have been possible. Davis, just shy of 50% of the vote in Part 1, might have had more votes cast favoring him than all the votes cast for all the candidates in Part 2, simply if more than half of the voters who voted in Part 1 failed to vote in Part 2. Those who cast a vote in Part 1 in the actual election were greater in number than those who cast a vote in Part 2, by an amount that turned out to be much smaller than 50 percent. Expressed as a percent of the total votes cast in part1, it was a mere 3.8%.

Of the votes cast in Part 2, Arnold Schwarzenegger captured a healthy plurality, 48.6%. It is reasonable to assume that the voters of California realized that in order to have a popularly elected governor rather than someone selected with little public approval as the result of a ridiculously quirky ballot process, they would somehow have to be in good agreement on who should replace Davis. Somehow, they were. After election day, political analysts and pundits explained to the world how, all things considered, Schwarzenegger really was quite a good choice, but none explained how the public had come together, only in the last week of the election, in apparent agreement on voting for his candidacy. Shelley and the 58 California county supervisors of elections were saved from a real fiasco by what could be called the "wisdom of the people". They should be grateful.

The officials had to make sure, county by county, that on short notice there would be enough voting machines to handle what could be, and indeed was, a large turn-out. Eleven different makes and models of machines were certified as acceptable by Shelley, and each county quickly had to acquire and deploy a huge number of them and train precinct recruiters how to guide voters through the process. The officials received the support of an organization www.votewatch.org that trained volunteers on proper voting procedures to assist at precincts throughout the state, in preparation for going national with a similar service for the 2004 elections.

The Office of the Secretary of State developed a magnificent central website (www.ss.ca.gov). One lengthy page gave the characteristics and specifications of the certified voting machines and data on how they were arrayed county by county. Each county supervisor of elections, starting at the close of the election on Oct. 7, reported to the central website the current available totals of votes for both parts of the ballot (and two referenda also on the ballot following Part 2) – including votes cast in three unusual categories in a manner never before used in a large election. Any voter could vote at any precinct even if the voter was not accepted as being registered at that precinct, and such votes would be tallied in a "provisional" category in the county. "Unprocessed absentee" ballots were kept in an "absentee" category. A third category, labeled "destroyed ballots", was fortunately inconsequentially small. When a provisional voter offered acceptable proof that s/he indeed should have been allowed to vote, that vote

120   – Ch.13–

was added to the "provisional" category displayed on the appropriate page of the central website. Absentee and destroyed ballots were handled in a similar manner.

The total votes for the yes/no question of Part 1 and for each of the 163 candidates of Part 2, were displayed automatically updated every few minutes, 24 hours a day, from Oct. 7 to Nov. 14. Any media observer – or interested person around the world – could access the website and see these latest totals slowly climb over the 38 day period, while percentages of the total vote changed amazingly little, less than ±0.1%.

The final votes were certified by Shelley in a way strange to all of us familiar with statewide polls, especially elections that got as much media coverage as this one. Though virtually everybody believed that Schwarzenegger was the governor-elect, nowhere did the certification state that. One could deduce who was governor-elect from looking at the data. The percentages showed that Schwarzenegger's total exceeded that of Davis and the other leading candidates. But nowhere to be seen was the total number of votes of all 163 candidates, nor accurate percentages for many minor candidates. It is almost as if Shelley had told those preparing the certification documents, "Don't add up the totals or figure the percentages for all the minor candidates. They're not necessary and you might make a mistake. Those numbers could not change the outcome. No one could lodge a significant complaint. Don't bother getting them accurate." There was no bias visible in Shelley's operation or documentation.

What a contrast to Florida's secretary of state in 2000, Katherine Harris who twice on TV joyfully announced George W. Bush the winner in Florida by a paper thin margin and thereby nationally by a single electoral vote. Harris was biased by her widely-known Republican activism in the campaign and made no apologies for these election follies that were her department's responsibility:

   – The butterfly ballot, which did not link the name in a straight line to the check-box for the candidate.

— Printed advice on ballots that if followed would void the ballot. Example, "Be sure to vote on every page."

— Over 40,000 ballots cast but mysteriously never counted.

— Registered voters prevented from voting when incorrectly told that they were not registered.

— A massive campaign conducted by Harris to remove thousands of names from voting lists throughout Florida for dubious reasons, e.g. having names similar to the name of someone who might have once been convicted of what was a misdemeanor, but later made a felony under Florida law.

After going to enormous lengths to run an unbiased election with a full 38 days to get the votes properly counted and the counts announced accurate to a single vote, Shelley had made an enormous and successful effort to avoid the Harris follies. The last thing that Shelley or anyone else in California of either party wanted was a repeat production.

The fundamental flaw of the California recall election was the two-part ballot. Of those voting in Part 1, 44.6% favored Davis. Of those voting in Part 2, 48.6% favored Schwarzenegger, and Schwarzenegger was the second choice of any voter who had already voted for Davis in Part 1. If 198,465 or more voters voted "no" in Part 1 and for Schwarzenegger in Part 2, then it would be true that based on first choice only, Davis had more votes than Schwarzenegger. If this were true, then, in the name of majority rule in a democracy, Davis should have been the winner and remained in office. The magic number, 198,465, was small, only 5.0% of the total pro-Davis vote. A full analysis showed that it is almost certain that the true desire of the majority of voters was to retain Davis as governor. The tiny uncertainty could easily have been eliminated by any recount that found 198,465 or more of those voting "no" in Part 1 and "Schwarzenegger" in Part 2. The rules laid down by the California courts prevented the recount, and thereby ignored the will of the majority and produced a failure of democracy. These conclusions are unaffected by the fact that from Oct. 8 on, probably no one had expected that Davis would remain as governor, even those few who may believe, as I do, that Davis was the voters' first choice.

Three aspects of the ballots: design, instructions and layout for both California 2003 and Florida 2000 were bad and thwarted the will of the people. Thus, despite all the effort to avoid a Florida-like fiasco, California has been tarred by the same brush. To be fair to the individuals responsible, Harris should be covered with tar from head to toe; and Shelley, well, should have a little dab on his new white suit.

Why do I see things this way and almost nobody else does? I have had years of experience, often in collaboration with the best pollsters in the United States, designing, conducting and analyzing polls where the public was asked to choose the most favored from a bunch of choices offered. The choices could be for the favorite among policy proposals, election candidates, or whatever. The outcome is most reliable if the choices are all offered in the same frame.

A simple example illustrates why. Suppose a poll offers just three response choices, A, B, and C, which happen to be related in a not uncommon way, known as "cyclical preference." This means that A is preferred over B, B is preferred over C, and C is preferred over A. If two questions are used, the first, A matched against B; and the second, the preferred A of the first question matched against C, then C becomes the most preferred of the three. Or put more generally, the choice that is tested only in the second question always wins. This, of course, is paradoxical, and impractical nonsense. The simple solution is to ask the public with all choices in a single question, "Which in a three-way match (and a level playing field) is preferred, A, B, or C?" The public will easily make its choice. The California recall election, commendable as it was in many ways, should not have had two parts.

The most compelling, detailed analysis of potential national election corruption appeared in an article by Bob Fitrakis of the Columbus Free Press, "Diebold, Electronic Voting and the Vast Right Wing Conspiracy", no longer available on the website of truthout.org.

Conclusions

"The Crisis of the 2004 Election", was described in the opening of this book (pp. 5-6). The spin – or lies – spun by politicians, their advisors, their financial backers, and the mainstream media, examined in all its dimensions in the first three chapters, has created not just a struggle, but an unholy, crazy war of the elites versus the people. This war has developed slowly over decades allowing clever pundits and politicians to make the case that the horrible stories of injustice and violence, whether presented in gory detail by the media or by the injustices and violence that many of us have witnessed first hand, are normal or no worse than in the past.

It is true that we Americans have rallied time and again to overcome differences and failures, redirected the nation back on to the right track, and succeeded in recreating and sustaining an America that has been the envy of much of the world. In the current crisis, many may believe we will do so again. This time I am not so sure. Why?

Knowingly or not, the elites have dis-empowered 99+% of the general public in a way that has pushed almost all of us into believing that we, the people, are collectively uninformed, mis-informed, dis-interested or incapable of agreeing on almost any coherent course of action without the involvement, the support, and acceptance of a large measure of control by the elites.

Good polling, particularly public-interest polling, shows almost the opposite is true. At consensus levels (over 67+%) the general public (and voters) – when presented with a wide range of choices in well-designed polls favor specific legislation and regulation in all the major issue areas:

o globalization,   o health care   o terrorism, o immigration/outsourcing
o education,   o the environment,   o national and homeland security,
o jobs   o economic opportunities   o goals and indicators.

The preferred choices of the people are consistent, persistent and resistant to counter-arguments and can make this a far better country **for all** than it has ever been in modern times.

The nature of the 2004 election crisis is much more dangerous than is generally understood, in part because that nature cannot be known precisely in advance. Futurists have been studying a long list of likely crisis possibilities for years. Crises may occur in a number of realms, such as the **collapse** of

- o government services
- o commercial services,
- o civil rights/liberties
- o international financial system,
- o the dollar

or by

- o major armed militia attacks,
- o new wars and insurrections,
- o environmental disasters,
- o giant terrorist attacks,
- o irretrievable vote counting breakdowns,

and likely, **in some sequence**, several of the above.

Even within each realm there are a large variety of possibilities. Well in advance, no specific major crisis development can be predicted until it suddenly looms. Nobody, neither public nor elites want to do anything but resolve any such crisis, whatever its nature turns out to be. These crises can be contained or overcome if only by postponing or forestalling the consequences of past failures, mistakes and mis-steps. This is what Americans have done in the past and I do not doubt can do again.

The weakest part of the chain of action that will be able to accomplish this recovery, is the lack of confidence that the American people have in the fact that we the people when presented with the major relevant facts all want to move in the same right direction and good polling shows can agree on how to do that.

The developments, following from the forces let loose by past bad elite decisions, will likely come fast and thick in the months ahead and, in truth-is-stranger-than-fiction fashion, might lead to wiping out democracy by dishonest political actions, particularly the 2004 national election itself. Knowing how to spot the spin enables each of us to react quickly to support whatever potential appears for righting the situation to get the nation moving in the right-direction recovery-mode, leading to erecting a structure that supports our democracy rather than destroying it. Your understanding will help. Follow the polls on the issues and the candidate races and be prepared to respond quickly to looming disasters to help save our wonderful country.

Index

ISBN 141202547-8